Boyband

Peter Quilter

A SAMUEL FRENCH ACTING EDITION

SAMUEL FRENCH

FOUNDED 1830

SAMUELFRENCH-LONDON.CO.UK
SAMUELFRENCH.COM

ISBN 978-0-573-01955-5

www.samuelfrench-london.co.uk

www.samuelfrench.com

FOR AMATEUR PRODUCTION ENQUIRIES

UNITED KINGDOM AND WORLD
EXCLUDING NORTH AMERICA
plays@SamuelFrench-London.co.uk
020 7255 4302/01

Each title is subject to availability from Samuel French,

depending upon country of performance.

BOYBAND

An early version of *BoyBand* was first presented at the Palace Theatre, Westcliff in May 1997. The production was directed by Christopher Dunham and starred Paul Keating and Nigel Harman.

BoyBand was fully revised and the show in its present form was first presented by PW Productions Ltd (Andrew Empson) and Adam Spigel Productions Ltd at the Derby Playhouse in April 1999. The show subsequently transferred to the Gielgud Theatre, Shaftesbury Avenue, London in May 1999 with the following cast:

Wayland	Bryan Murray
Sean	Damien Flood
Danny	Daniel Crossley
Matt	Tom Ashton
Jay	Stepps
Adam	Kevin Andrew
Robert	William Oxborrow
Mandy	Caroline Head
Various female roles	Hayley Tamaddon
Various female roles	Kelly Morris
First cover to the band	Richard Taylor Woods

Directed by Peter Rowe
Choreographed by Emma Victoria
Music Supervisor, Tina Matthews
Designed by Andrew Leigh
Lighting design by Chris Ellis
Sound design by Sebastian Frost

CHARACTERS

MEMBERS OF THE BOYBAND
Sean
Danny
Matt
Jay
Adam

Wayland: the manager
Robert: the PR consultant
Mandy: the choreographer

VARIOUS FEMALE ROLES, PLAYED BY TWO ACTRESSES
Laura: a schoolgirl
Debbie: a schoolgirl
Anna: a photographer
Reporter
TOTP presenter
Camera operators
Floor Manager
Photographer
Backing dancers

The action takes place within the setting of a concert arena

Time — 1996 or can be up-dated to a contemporary setting

PRODUCTION NOTES

PRODUCTIONS NOT ABLE TO USE VIDEO
All the detailed video sequences can be replaced with slide projections and audio/radio pieces. Please refer to the "Alternatives to Video Plot" page 70.

BACKING MUSIC
The original West End producers are able to lease out the backing music for all the songs. This means you will need superb sound equipment rather than a superb band. Please see "Music Notes" on page vii for further details.

SONG SELECTION
The songs detailed within the text are those that were used in the original West End production of the show. However it is also permitted to select your own choice of song material and find/create your own backing music or band scores. Note that any pre-existing song material has to receive copyright clearance from PRS (or other national organisations representing music copyright) before it can be used.

LOCATION
Productions are at liberty to localise the show, making references to places/venues relevant to the country of production. Certain verbal terms, for example "friend of Dorothy", in UNIT 23 can also be altered if a better-understood/funnier alternative is available in a local language. The same is true for the general language of the boys, which must always be young and streetwise — so current slang and contemporary modes of speech can be used at appropriate moments. Note that the show can either be set in 1996, or updated to the present day.

SCENE CHANGE
For much of the time, *BoyBand* is a fast-moving, high-energy show and the scene changes should reflect this. They should be minimal, crisp and quick.

COSTUME
The costume should illustrate the increasing success of the band. The boys' outfits should therefore start out cheap and gradually become more chic and expensive. Wayland's costumes should also reflect his growing income levels, though he never has particularly good taste.

MICROPHONES
The need to sing and dance against a backing track will be likely to demand special personal microphones, which can easily be hired. Most of the original productions used small microphones that came over the mouth and clipped over one ear. These were found to be practical and unobtrusive and were small enough that they could be worn during most of the scenes as well as the song numbers.

Peter Quilter

MUSIC NOTES

For use of the original West End production backing music please address all intial inquiries to the Editorial Department, Samuel French Ltd.

The song "Driving Me Crazy" created for the European tour, is available from MELODY MUSICAL PRODUCTIONS, Mark Vijn, Acherom 79-E, 1621 KS Hoorn, Netherlands, via a separate licence.

Other plays by Peter Quilter
published by
Samuel French Ltd

Respecting Your Piers
The Canterville Ghost (adapted from the story by Oscar Wilde)

ACT I

The stage is in darkness. Unseen as yet is the setting of a concert arena. There is a vast concert lighting rig and a giant video wall at the back of the stage. Within this frame, settings should be kept minimal and simple

Voice-over And now — at Wembley ... Please welcome Britain's number one boy band — "Freedom!"

There is the sound of screams and hysteria from a Wembley crowd. Music. This is a full concert sequence — moving lights, pyros, special effects, etc. A slick, impressive state of the art gig

   Backing dancers perform in a background group

   The band make a dramatic, heavily stylized entrance. They are wearing expensive, stylish, designer clothes

Sean sings lead vocal

The screen reads "FREEDOM"

Song No. 1 — Set Me Free

At the end of the number the boys stand on Mic to address the audience

Sean Hallo, Wembley!
Danny It's brilliant to be here.
Jay This is a special show because tonight ——
Adam — we're going to reveal — everything!
Matt You're going to see bits of us that you have never seen before!
Danny Tonight — we're gonna give you the naked truth.
Jay There's been a lot of stories in the press.
Adam Some people said we'd never be seen on stage together again.
Matt But we made it ——
Danny Just.
Sean And now it's our chance to tell you what really happened ——

Adam To go back to the beginning ——
Danny When "Freedom" was just a glint in a manager's eye …

Black-out

Music

UNIT 2

The video screen shows an advertisement in a newspaper stating "Open auditions for a new boyband, Saturday 10 a.m. at Danceworks". The screen fades out as lights rise on Jay and Matt

Music continues to underscore

Jay and Matt are marking the final moves of a dance routine. They are wearing cheaper and grubbier clothes than in UNIT 1. *This is their audition for the band. They are observed by Wayland and Mandy*

The music ends and Jay and Matt finish the short routine

Wayland Thank you, Jay, Matt. How many times have we seen you now?
Jay Seven.
Matt Yeah — this was the seventh.
Wayland Well, I know you gave it your best shot, but you won't be coming back for any more ——

Jay and Matt look dejected

— because you've got the job!
Matt What?
Jay You mean we're in?
Wayland Welcome to the band!

Jay and Matt are overjoyed

Sean, Danny and Adam enter and go over to congratulate Jay and Matt

Introductions: this is Sean, he sings the lead on most of the songs. This is Danny, he writes most of the songs; and this is Adam, he … Well, this is Adam.

Mandy brings over a contract attached to a clipboard

My associate, Mandy, you already know. (*He takes the contract and holds it up*) Now listen up. This is your contract. Everyone gets the same deal and it's non-negotiable. So I want to explain exactly what I'm offering here before you decide whether this is something that you want or not. Now listen very carefully. This band — your band — will be called "Freedom". I'll pay each of you a hundred pounds a week until we cut the third album. When that album is released, you get a full percentage — that's the point we all get rich. Until then, you get nothing. Why? Transport, hotels, clothes, venues, promotion, studios — I'm paying for the lot. I'm going to invest a ton of money in you lads, and everything we make back, I'm going to plough straight back into promoting the band. I'm doing this because I believe in you boys; I believe in "Freedom." I'm committing everything to this project and I'm asking you to do the same. Now if you can't, that's fine. There are plenty of other boys out there who'll be only too glad to take your place. But once you sign this contract, you agree to do exactly as I say. All decisions regarding your professional and your social lives will be made by me. If you can't live with that, if you don't trust me, if you can't respect me — now is the time to walk. (*He takes a pen from his pocket*) Here's a pen, there's the door. All or nothing ... You sign at the bottom.

The boys all grab at the pen simultaneously. Wayland smiles victoriously

Black-out

Unit 3

Unseen as yet is the setting for a rehearsal studio. There is a cassette player

Music

A series of photographs and video clips of the five guys at various stages in their childhood is shown as a video sequence. We see them as babies, then as children, then as teenagers and then as young people. The final image is a contemporary portrait of each of them. The word "Freedom" stretches across the screens

The Lights come up on the rehearsal studio

*Music plays from the cassette player (**Song No. 2 — We Got it All**). The boys are rehearsing a routine with their choreographer, Mandy. They mark the routine with reasonable competence, but with no passion. Matt smiles throughout. Mandy demonstrates the moves, vocalizing each gesture. The boys follow her. Danny is distracted for a moment*

Mandy Danny, have you got a problem?
Danny No.
Mandy Then concentrate and stop farting about.

They continue for a few more moments

OK, now come on — keep it sexy — Matt! You have to stop smiling occasionally.
Matt I can't help it. I'm just happy to be here.
Mandy Just remember, Matt — smouldering, full of lust — not looking like you've just won a *Blue Peter* badge!
Matt I'll try. Sorry.

The boys try a few more moves

Mandy (*with exasperation*) Guys, guys! I'm not getting the sex.
Adam Well maybe you should get out more often.

They laugh

Wayland enters. He stops the cassette player

Wayland Well, it's nice to see you all having such a good time — on my money. Listen up — I've just booked you in for your first live gig. This Friday — a ten minute spot, two numbers, performing to a crowd of at least a hundred. There, that's wiped the smile off your faces.
Sean What's the venue, boss?
Wayland You remember I told you this band is going all the way to the top?
Danny Yeah ——
Wayland Well, on Friday — we start at the bottom.

Black-out

Unit 4

A girls' school in South London

The school hall is dimly lit. There is a naff tinsel curtain as a backdrop

The following announcement is delivered over the school sound system complete with feedback, etc. It is muddled, monotone and naff. During the announcement two girls in school uniforms, Laura and Debbie, set up five microphone stands, one of which they forget to raise to the correct height

Announcer/teacher And now, a very special treat for all in year nine —
because this band has never appeared in public before. So we're very lucky
to have them here at Charlton Comprehensive. Let's give a warm welcome
to the world premiére of — "Freedom".

Full lights come up

*The boys enter, one by one. Each of them wears a white T-shirt with their
own name printed on the front and the "Freedom" logo on the back. Adam
wears his T-shirt back-to-front*

The boys perform the number they rehearsed earlier in UNIT *3. They use
hand- held microphones with long extension leads. Sean sings lead vocal.
They perform with enthusiasm, but it all becomes a bit of a mess. Adam's T-
shirt mistake is realized at one choreographic point when all the boys turn
us. When they do a cross-over, Sean ends up tangled amongst the microphone
wires and Jay spends much of the song trying to cope with a microphone
stand that has been set at the level of his waist. Matt smiles throughout.
Though not perfect, the performance still shows great potential*

Song No. 2 — We Got It All

Black-out

There is the sound of hundreds of screaming girls

UNIT 5

*The toilets at the school, which are being used by the band as their changing-
room*

The boys enter from the performance

Danny I can't believe we got through it.
Matt Did you hear them screaming?
Jay It's so cool to have finally done it.
Adam You got any deodorant, Jay?
Jay Yeah. You want to borrow some?
Adam No, I was just asking, 'cos I could smell your armpits from half-way
down the corridor.

Jay sniffs his own armpit

Jay It's not that bad.

Adam Jay — you make the bog smell fresh.

Wayland enters

Wayland (*elated*) Great start, boys. We're going all the way to the top; success is in the air, I can smell it.
Adam No, that'll be Jay's armpits.
Matt It went really well, didn't it?
Wayland Those girls were crazy about you.
Sean So how many more of these schools do we need to do, boss?
Wayland None. We're going to by-pass all those, Sean. We're ready to move up a few stages, start playing the clubs.
Danny Already?
Matt Do you think we'll go down all right?
Wayland If you put the work in. Now, I'm gonna set up a proper showcase — one of the London clubs. And once we launch the band properly, you'll have a lot of press and promotional work to do.
Matt I'll be crap at that — I won't know what to say.
Wayland Don't worry, Matt — I'll look after you. I'll set up some sessions on how to present yourself in front of the cameras, and how to handle the fans — because, believe me, if that show was anything to go by, they're gonna give you a lot of attention.
Jay Yeah, man, I'm gonna be a sex god!
Wayland On the subject of sex — remember your contract; no sex unless I say so. The reason those girls will be screaming for you is that each one of them believes they're in with a chance. So you have to stay available. Your being single is vital to the marketing campaign, so no-one here — no-one — is to screw that up.

Mandy enters

Mandy Can I come in?
Adam Sure, have a seat.(*He raises a toilet seat*)
Mandy Well done, boys, that was fantastic.
All Thanks, Mandy, cheers, (*etc.*)
Mandy (*to Wayland*) You happy?
Wayland Happy? I passed happy when the girls started fainting. I'm ecstatic. OK, boys, I need a quick word with Mandy. You get changed and I'll see you back in the van. (*He throws Sean the van keys*) It's parked outside the gates.

Wayland leads Mandy out of the scene. The Lights cross-fade to a spot-light on Mandy and Wayland

Mandy Where are we going? Behind the bike sheds?

Wayland This is it, Mandy. This is the one that's gonna make us millions.

Mandy You've said that about every band you've ever signed. Even that cheesy girl group — the one with the swimming costumes. I remember the speech; "I believe in you girls, I believe in 'Bikini'."

Wayland This is different. Those five boys are the perfect combination. You saw the reaction out there. They look great together, they can move ——

Mandy More or less.

Wayland They can even sing, for Christ's sake — when did you ever hear of a boyband that could actually sing! If we package them properly and give them the right launch, they're going to be unstoppable.

Mandy Well I hope you're right. About time you had a bit of luck.

Wayland Luck's got nothing to do with it. I just finally got the formula right. Now, I want to cancel the rest of the schools.

Mandy All of them?

Wayland I'm going to set up a proper showcase — one of the clubs in London. Fifteen minutes at least. That means two more numbers.

Mandy When?

Wayland End of next week.

Mandy You've gotta be joking! I have got other work, you know.

Wayland Cancel it. I don't like the idea of you working for other people. Why don't come and work for me full time?

Mandy Really?

Wayland Yeah, I want you on the team. I think we're the perfect combination. Don't you? (*He embraces Mandy from behind*)

Mandy Well, I'm willing to give it a go. Those boys really could be good.

Wayland Yeah — this could be your big break.

Mandy *My* big break?

Wayland lets go of the embrace

Wayland OK — to buisness; I'm going to need someone to handle the press and PR.

Mandy I know a guy — he's very good.

Wayland Yeah?

Mandy He's at EMI, but he might fancy working for a smaller outfit.

Wayland Give him a call.

Mandy He won't be cheap.

Wayland I'll sort out the money.

Mandy Oh yeah — how?

Wayland I don't know — I'll sell my flat if I have to. I'll see you at the office tomorrow. Oh — and Mandy — call at the chemist's on the way in.

Mandy What for?

Wayland Wax.

Mandy Wax?

Wayland Jay's got a few hairs coming through. (*He mimes ripping hair off his chest, making the appropriate sound effects*)

UNIT 6

Unseen as yet is the setting for a venue — "The Rainbow Club", London

The following dialogue is shown as a video sequence. It is Sean's practice screen test. All the boys sit on a couch. The camera's focus is on Sean

Wayland (*voice only*) Just be natural and relaxed. Look right into the lens and talk about yourself. OK? Sean, you go first.

Sean Hi, I'm Sean and I've been working in the music business for about five years now, mostly as a solo artist ——

Danny Solo piss artist.

Sean I've done the UK circuit and a lot of international touring.

Adam Cross Channel Ferries.

Sean Let me tell you a bit about my new band.

Danny looks very unhappy at this comment

We're called "Freedom" and though we've only been together for a few weeks, we've already been booked into a major London venue. I sing lead on most of the songs and it's been going pretty well so far. My dad said I was always destined to be ——

Danny (*moving directly in front of the camera*) And now the weather — despite the fact that Sean thinks the sun shines out of his arse, it will in fact be pissing down.

Sean tries to push his way back to the front. They all end up tumbling off the couch and on to the floor

The screen goes to black-out

Announcer (*voice only, with a cool laid -back voice*) And now we have a very special treat for you here at "The Rainbow Club". Making their first appearance in central London, please give it up for — "Freedom".

The Lights come up on the band

All the band are dressed in white

Danny sings lead vocal

Song No. 3 — My T Love

Black-out

Unit 7

A photographic studio. There are cameras, tripods and flash umbrellas

Wayland is pacing impatiently. Mandy is in the background

Wayland What's he playing at, Mandy? I thought you said he was good.
Mandy He is good.
Wayland So why is he taking so long?

Robert enters

Robert, we've got to be out of here by two.
Robert There's a problem. Anna, the photographer — she's refusing to go ahead with the shoot.
Wayland What!?
Robert She insists on being paid now — in cash.
Wayland She can forget that.
Robert She says she's worked for you before. Some girls in swimsuits ...?
Wayland (*realizing*) Oh ...Yeah ...
Robert Apparently, you still owe her five hundred quid.
Wayland OK — OK. (*He opens up a wallet, which is packed with notes. He counts out five hundred pounds and gives it to Robert*) Give her that and tell her to get her arse in here now.
Robert (*to Mandy*) Does he always do business like this?
Mandy You'll get used to it.
Robert (*to Wayland*) What about the stylist?
Wayland He can wait for his!

Robert exits

Wayland puts his wallet away

Mandy (*observing Wayland*) Have you signed the record deal?
Wayland No. I'm holding out for a bigger advance.
Mandy So where did the cash come from?
Wayland A bridging facility to ease the cash flow situation.

Mandy (*realizing*) You've sold your flat!?
Wayland I'll stick my bed in the back room at the office.
Mandy Bloody hell, Wayland!
Wayland It's only temporary. Once we get some exposure for the band, those record companies will be gagging for us. Now, go and see what that stylist is putting them into. And remember — I want to see flesh, lots of flesh.

Mandy exits. Robert and Anna enter

Robert This is Anna. I believe you've already met?
Wayland Oh yes, yes. Well — now that your pockets are full, can we make a start?
Anna Ready when you are.
Wayland This is for the "Freedom Press Pack." So, I need six good colour shots and four black and white — and they have to be sexy, very sexy.
Robert I think Anna knows what's required.
Wayland (*short*) Robert, will you get the boys out here. We're really running late now.

Robert walks to the side of the stage and calls the boys in

Robert Guys! Let's go — we've got to do this now.

The boys enter and edge cautiously on stage, wearing only minimal, sexy undergarments. They are highly embarrassed

Wayland Good, lovely.
Sean Do we really have to do this? This is embarrassing.
Wayland Why?
Sean Why! Look at me!
Anna You look great.

The boys realize the photographer is a woman and, with a vocal reaction — "Oh, my God, it's a woman", etc. — they immediately turn their backs and huddle in a corner

Wayland You all wanted to be sex gods.
Matt Can we change our minds?
Wayland Come on, get on with it.
Anna OK, guys, just get into a line for me.

Reluctantly, the boys get into a line in front of the camera. Their hands are clasped over their crotches, like a football team protecting goal at a free kick

Anna Right ... OK. Let's get rid of these hands, shall we? (*She manoeuvres the boys into new positions*) Arms round each other's shoulders. That's better. Now, look straight at the camera. Imagine it's a beautiful woman and you want to make love to her all night.
Adam Will she settle for twenty minutes?
Anna OK — now let's give that sexy look a try.

Each of the boys muster their best sexy look. Matt smiles broadly

The one on the end; what's your name?
Matt Matt.
Anna Matt. Stop smiling.

The other boys look at Matt

Matt Sorry, guys. (*He gives his sexiest look*)

The others then do the same

Anna OK — that's good! Hold that ——

The camera flashes several times in quick succession

Black-out

The video screen lights up

Music

Unit 8

Unseen as yet is the setting for a television studio

A video sequence shows a montage of various studio photo shots of the boys in boisterous poses; striking, sexy and in various states of undress

The Lights rise on the television studio

Mandy and Robert are present, plus the Floor Manager and other people in the background

Wayland enters

Wayland We'll have to do another take. Matt was out of step.

Floor Manager That doesn't matter — we can cut away from that.

Wayland No. I won't compromise — not on the promo for the band's first single — it's too important.

Floor Manager But you've got hours of material by now ——

Wayland Who gives a shit? I've booked this studio till two a.m. — and I want another take. Mandy, go and get the boys.

Floor Manager Oh, for God's sake!

Robert steps calmly into the fray

Robert Claire, we want one clean take, right through. That's the whole point. It's got to feel live and immediate. If it's full of cut-aways and edits, it won't work. It has to be one continuous shot. I know it's a difficult thing to achieve, but that's why we came to you guys in the first place.

Floor Manager ... OK, Robert.

Robert Thank you.

Floor Manager We're going again, studio.

Wayland gives Robert a thumbs up

The boys enter, ready for the shoot. Jay is listening to a radio and has it to his ear

Wayland Now come on, guys — let's get this right or we'll be here all night. I want you all to concentrate.

Jay (*a loud yell*) Yeesss!!

Wayland What?

Jay Manchester United won two-nil.

Wayland (*charging at Jay*) Give me that ——

Mandy (*stepping in*) It's all right, I'll take it.

Mandy takes the radio from Jay before Wayland gets to it. Wayland stares at Jay in disbelief

Wayland Concentrate!

Floor Manager Clear the floor, please.

Wayland And Matt — try and think of something sad — OK?

Matt Sorry. Sorry, guys.

Floor Manager Starting positions.

Wayland exits. Everyone else exits apart from the boys

(*Voice only, off*) Stand-by studio. We're rolling. When you're ready, guys.

Lights focus on the boys as they get into their opening positions

Sean sings lead vocal

Song No. 4 — How Will I Know?

At the end of the song, the boys freeze in position

The Floor Manager enters

Floor Manager He's happy with that one, guys. That's a wrap—thank you.

The boys relax

Wayland enters

Wayland That's more like it! And that's confirmed it — "How Will I Know?" is gonna be our first single.
Matt Danny — that's one of yours, you'll get royalties.
Wayland No, he won't. He doesn't see a penny till the third album, just like everyone else.

Robert enters and hands out tour schedules

Wayland Now, we've got a big tour lined up to promote the single. This is the schedule and I'm warning you — it's really tight.
Danny Bit like you then, Wayland.
Wayland (*not amused*) This is where it gets serious, Danny. You won't see your families for a while and the only time you won't see me is when you're asleep. By the way, you get just seven hours a night — that's in there as well.
Danny Where does it tell us when to piss?
Wayland (*with anger*) Just get changed — OK?

Wayland exits with Robert

Matt Danny, what did you say that for? You were getting his back up.
Danny (*holding out the schedule*) Have you seen this? I signed up for a boy band, not a borstal.
Sean Obviously, you don't know how the music business works.
Danny Then I guess I'll just bow to your superior knowledge, oh mighty one.
Sean Don't be a prat.
Jay All right, guys, calm down — it's been a long day.

Matt Yeah, Danny, don't forget how lucky we are to have all this.

Wayland enters

Wayland Oi! What is this? We're waiting for you lot — get a move on.

The boys exit

Wayland grabs Sean as he passes

Wayland Sean, can I have a word?
Sean Yeah, sure, boss.
Wayland What's all this I hear about you and Anna?
Sean Anna?
Wayland Anna — the photographer. I hear you've been keeping in touch.
Sean All I did was phone her. How the hell did you find out about that?
Wayland I find out about everything, Sean. Haven't you worked that out yet? I'm disappointed in you. I thought I could rely on you to be professional.
Sean Oh, come on, Wayland. All that "no girlfriends" stuff is fine for the others but — you know me, I can be discreet.
Wayland No, Sean. The rules are the same for all of you.
Sean Look, in all the gigs I've done for you, have I ever caused you any grief?
Wayland This is different — this isn't just another gig.
Sean But no-one will ever know.
Wayland Are you not hearing me? I said "No."
Sean Oh, for God's sake ——
Wayland Listen, do you want to go back to making a fool of yourself on the ferries?
Sean No.
Wayland Singing "Summer Holiday" to pissed up pensioners all the way from Portsmouth to Cherbourg. Because you can, you know. I'll book you on next week, if that's what you want.
Sean Of course I don't.
Wayland Don't test me, Sean. You'll come out a loser. I've got too much money riding on this operation and I will not have it ruined by your dick. Now in the not too distant future, you're gonna have a great solo career, and when that time comes — you can jump into bed with whatever girl, woman or farm animal your heart desires. But right now you keep it zipped.
Sean You're really serious about this, aren't you?
Wayland You've finally got it. Now go and join the others.

Robert enters. Sean exits

Robert Problem?
Wayland Just keep a close eye on them. I don't want them to even breathe without me hearing about it. There's got to be absolute control, or I can't make this work.
Robert Sure.
Wayland Single goes out Monday.
Robert I hope it charts.
Wayland Oh, it'll chart all right.
Robert What makes you so sure?
Wayland Because I know you'll be out there buying as many copies as it takes.

With a smile, Wayland exits

Black-out

UNIT 9

Unseen as yet is the setting for a hotel suite. There is a TV set and video player, a radio, a telephone, a bottle of champagne and glasses and a plate of pathetic-looking sandwiches on a table

The following dialogue plays as a video sequence from MTV or a similar music channel

MTV Presenter (*directly to camera, in the casual European Pop TV style*) And welcome back to Boy Band Day on MTV. "Freedom" have become the latest pop sensation with their first single going straight into the top five on the UK charts. Their first major tour opened tonight in Manchester and from there we have Matt on the end of the line. Matt, can you hear me?
Matt (*voice only; shrouded by the crackles and fuzz of being on a phone line*) Yes I can.

The Lights rise dimly on the hotel setting. Matt is on the phone and Wayland is issuing instructions to him. The other boys are gathered around the TV set, reacting audibly to Matt's answers

MTV Presenter How did it go tonight?
Matt Excellent. We had a great crowd, it was unbelievable.
MTV Presenter So you're partying tonight, then?
Matt We'll be having a few drinks, but nothing major.
MTV Presenter Matt, what's it like having two thousand girls screaming at you?

Matt Oh it's, er — it's pretty cool.
MTV Presenter I bet. And you can see highlights of that "Freedom" concert here next month. But for now — thanks, Matt — and we'll be back right after this...

The video screen fades to black-out. The Lights rise fully on the hotel suite. As the Lights rise, Matt puts the phone down and they all applaud him. Robert switches off the TV

Matt How did I come across?
Adam Like Bambi with Parkinson's.

Laughter

Wayland Right, that's it. No more work today — time to celebrate! Robert, why don't you go and fetch the mail bag?

Robert exits

Wayland pops open the bottle of champagne and pours it into glasses

I want to tell you guys that you were fantastic on stage tonight. We've got a single in the charts, a tour on the road, and every branch of the media banging on my door. I can't wait for the release of the album — it's gonna be enormous. So, here's to you guys. Bloody well done!

They toast their glasses

Right — get stuck into the food, it cost me a fortune. (*He gestures to the plate of sandwiches*)
Danny Cheese sandwiches, Wayland. You've surpassed yourself this time.

The boys eat, drink and chat

Robert enters, carrying a huge bag of mail

Wayland Thanks, Robert. Boys — here's your post!

Robert empties the contents of the mail bag on to the floor. Out tip hundreds of letters, gifts, cards and cuddly toys, including a Mickey Mouse and a Teletubby. The boys immediately dive in looking for items addressed to themselves. Jay is first to find something — a Manchester United scarf

Jay Someone's sent me a Man. United scarf. (*Reading a label on the scarf aloud*) "Dear Jay. Please wear this as a token of our love." Cool. (*He puts the scarf on; reading*) "If I ever see anyone else kissing you, I'll murder them". (*Horrified, he quickly takes the scarf off and chucks it back into the pile*)

Matt Whose is that Mickey Mouse? Is it mine?

Sean checks out the label on the Mickey Mouse

Sean Hard luck, sucker, it's addressed to me.

Matt (*picking up the Teletubby*) I'll swap it for this Teletubby.

Sean Not a chance. What else you got?

Danny (*reading from a letter*) "Dear Danny, I am sending you a pair of my knickers". (*He takes a pair of frilly girl's knickers from the envelope and stares at them*) Well that's a bit stupid. They're not gonna fit me are they? (*He puts the knickers over his head instead*)

Wayland enjoys the moment. He then heads into a distant corner of the room to make a phone call

Matt (*finding a diary*) Some girl's given me her diary!

Jay (*finding a photo*) This one's sent me a photo of her dog.

Danny looks over Jay's shoulder

Danny No, that's *her*! (*He takes up another photo*) Here's the photo of the dog!

Laughter

Sean Robert, how do they know we're staying here?

Robert The fans find out your every move. You'll get used to that.

Adam (*holding a letter in the air*) OK. Hold it everyone. This is it. (*He stands proudly reading out the letter*) "Dear Adam, why don't the two of us get together? I know I can give you the time of your life. What do you say, sexy? Love from ——" (*he turns the page over*) "— Barry!!"

They all laugh uproariously

Barry from Romford. He can forget it — I'm not going all the way to Romford!

There is more laughter

Sean has been sent an article from the "Daily Star" newspaper. He opens it out and reads it

Sean (*with shock*) What the hell is this?
Robert (*realizing*) Oh, Christ, give that to me.
Sean "My wild nights with 'Freedom''s sexy Sean".
Danny What's that?
Sean Some girl has gone and done an article about me. Talking about our bloody sex life! What she go and do that for?
Robert Money, Sean. Don't worry about it.
Sean What do you mean, "Don't worry about it?" Has anyone described your balls in a national paper?

Wayland notices the problem and cuts short the phone call

Wayland What's all this?
Robert He's got the *Daily Star* article.
Sean You knew about this?
Wayland Just give it here.
Sean Why didn't you tell me?
Wayland Let's just get rid of it. (*He snatches the article from Sean and stuffs it into his pocket*)
Sean And what's the point of that? It's not the only copy. Millions of people are reading about me screwing some old slapper on the floor of a Portakabin.
Danny Portakabin!?
Sean Shut it, Danny.
Wayland This stuff's going to happen. You've just got to laugh it off.
Sean (*suddenly realizing*) Oh shit! My mum gets that paper! She'll have read this. Her and half the country.
Adam Look on the bright side, at least they think you're straight! I'm getting mail from dodgy blokes in Romford!
Sean I don't think this is funny. I'd like to see how you lot would feel about it.

Sean storms off-stage

Wayland (*calling after Sean*) Where are you going? (*To Robert*) Robert, go and get him.

Robert runs off-stage after Sean

Danny Here, Wayland, how much would that girl have got paid for that article?

Wayland Three grand. (*Realizing, he covers his tracks*) ... Erm, I think it's — about three grand, more or less.

Danny So we get a hundred pounds a week for all this sweat and some bird is getting three thousand pounds for putting in print the size of Sean's todger?

Adam That's a thousand pounds an inch.

Danny Well, at that rate, I'd have got ten grand.

Wayland puts a video tape into the video cassette player

Wayland OK, time to get this party back on the tracks.

Jay What's that?

Wayland Matt's screen test.

Matt Oh no, please. Not again!

Wayland clicks on the video via a remote control. Matt hangs his head in embarrassment

Black-out

Unit 10

Unseen as yet is the setting for the TV programme, "Top of the Pops". There are TV cameras (etc.)

The following dialogue is shown as a video sequence. It is Matt's screen test. On screen, the other boys sit around Matt

Matt Hi, I'm Matt. (*He pauses*) What do I say now?

Jay Just talk.

Matt About what?

Sean What you did before the band, anything.

Matt I worked in a butcher's on Saturdays. I made the sausages.

Adam Give me strength!

Matt And I priced up the tins.

The boys groan and laugh

Matt Then at the end of the day I'd wipe down the counters.

Danny No please, I can't take any more!

On screen, they all bundle on top of Matt. Chaos

Adam (*amidst the bundle*) Here — he's still bloody smiling!

On screen, Matt's smiling face is revealed yet again

The screen fades out

A spotlight rises on a presenter for the TV programme "Top of the Pops". She is filmed "live" by a camera operator

The footage transfers immediately to the stage video screen

TOTP Presenter   The next band tonight are making their very first appearance on *Top of the Pops*. This is their new single taken from their best selling album and it's climbed this week all the way to number two. Please give it up for the deeply gorgeous — "Freedom!"

Full Lights come up on the band. The camera operator turns the camera on to the stage area and films the performance of the song. The boys perform on stage with the video film of their performance being relayed simultaneously on the screen

Sean sings lead vocal

Song No. 5 — Better Be Good

Black-out

Unit 11

Wayland's office. There are a desk and chairs. On the desk there is a telephone and a large rolled-up poster

Robert is in the office with Mandy and Wayland. Robert and Mandy try to make calls while Wayland is charging about

Wayland We've got to get more air time.
Mandy They've just done *Top of the Pops*.
Wayland We need more — a lot more. Has Abigail been in touch about the Lottery show?
Mandy Not yet.
Wayland Well that's just not good enough. Robert, why aren't we getting more air time?
Robert I'm trying.

Wayland Are you trying hard?

Robert Yes.

Wayland So why are you wasting time talking to me?

Robert I have no idea.

Wayland Get hold of Mark Rivers. I need to check the merchandising for next week. Nothing goes ahead till I've seen it. Not a badge, not a sticker, nothing. Where am I tomorrow morning?

Mandy Bank.

Wayland Oh Christ. Give them a ring. Say I'm in Germany.

Mandy You've already put it off twice.

Wayland I don't want to talk to them until we get the money in from Sheffield. (*He checks his watch*) I need to get to the studio. Anything else?

Mandy Yes. Lisa called.

Wayland Oh shit.

Robert Who's Lisa?

Mandy Ex-wife.

Wayland What did you tell her?

Mandy That you're in Germany.

Wayland (*with delight*) Good! Right — I'm off.

Robert You need to see the artwork for the poster.

Wayland What poster?

Robert The milk campaign.

Robert and Mandy hold up the huge poster of an advertisement for milk. The poster shows one of the band members, stripped to the waist and sweaty, with a towel draped round his shoulders. He is holding a glass of milk. The top caption reads, "Are you getting yours every day?"

Wayland That airbrush work's not good enough. You can see his spots. And why isn't there a "Freedom" logo on it? Call Alex and tell him to pull his finger out. Robert, you left your phone!

Robert I was showing you the ... Oh heaven help me. (*He returns to the phone and dials*)

Wayland Have you heard anything from Wickham's?

Mandy Not yet.

Wayland Well get hold of them — I need to know if the rig is gonna fit.

Mandy Whatever you say.

Wayland That's right. Whatever I say. You hear that Robert?

Robert No, I was on the phone.

Wayland Good! Progress!

Black-out

A video sequence shows a series of milk poster adverts, each showing a slightly different photo of the band member and each with a different caption — "Are you getting yours?", "Fancy it long and cool?", "Are you gagging for it?"

UNIT 12

A recording studio

The boys have earphones cupped over one ear and share the three micro-phones on stands. Danny carries some sheet music

They boys sing the final lines of a song — one to be performed later in the show. They pause

Robert (*voice only over the studio intercom*) OK, guys, just hang on for a minute.
Jay That's got to be the next single, Danny, it's a great song.
Danny Cheers, Jay. Three more to go and we'll have another album.

Adam ambles towards the door

Jay Oi — where are you going?
Adam They'll be ages. I'm going out for a smoke.
Sean Wayland's told you no cigarettes.
Adam I'm not going to have a cigarette.

Adam exits

Sean What's he playing at?
Danny Don't get involved. It's his decision.
Sean What's going on?
Matt As long as he's careful about it.
Sean Is he smoking dope?
Danny Sean, keep your voice down.
Sean He can't do that.
Danny Well he *is* doing it.
Sean If I can't have sex, he can't have a joint.
Jay Don't say anything to him 'cos it won't help.

Sean ignores Jay and walks out of the studio in search of Adam

Am I invisible or something? Didn't he hear what I just said?

Robert (*voice only over the studio intercom*) Thanks, guys. That was a really good one. You can take a break now.

Matt Excellent. (*To Danny*) Are you coming to eat?

Danny No, mate, there's some music I want to scribble down.

Matt God, Danny, you never stop.

Danny I've got no choice. If I wasn't writing songs, I'd still be working in a supermarket. (*He gives a cheeky look at Matt*) Or making sausages.

Danny exits as Mandy enters

Matt Jay?

Jay No, not right now — I need to talk to Mandy about something.

Matt I can't go to eat on my own — I'm gonna look like "Billy No-Mates".

Jay I won't be long, Matt.

Matt All right. I'll tell you what I'm gonna do. I'll go and get some water, then I'll come back for you. (*He starts to exit, then turns back*) Shall I get you the football results?

Jay No — it doesn't matter.

Matt exits

Jay takes a twenty pound note out of his pocket and gives it to Mandy

Mandy Twenty quid?

Jay That's all I've got. Honest. Just tell them I'll try and save more next week.

Mandy Don't worry, I'll put in a bit extra for you myself.

Jay No, that's not fair.

Mandy Jay — what are they supposed to do? Just not feed the baby for a week? It's all right, I'll handle it.

Jay When did you last see them?

Mandy Sunday.

Jay How's she coping?

Mandy As well as any single mum with a young kid.

Jay (*with hurt*) She's not a single mum, Mandy! I can't help it if I can't be there.

Mandy I know that, Jay. It's just — they need to see you.

Jay And don't you think I want to see them? I'm watching my son grow up through photographs.

Mandy Well, I don't know when you're going to see them again. As soon as these sessions are finished you're back on the road. I've been booking the tour all week.

Jay What!? I thought he was gonna give us a break.

Mandy And God help us if Wayland ever finds out about this. Sometimes I wish I'd never got you that bloody audition.

Jay Oh, don't say that. Look, if we can just keep it going till the third album, Shelley and the kid will be set up for life.

Mandy Well, can you at least ring your mum?

Jay Yeah, I will.

Mandy It's not easy for her, you know. She's got Shelley and the baby cooped up in that little house, fans pestering her every time she steps outside ——

Jay Mandy, I'll call her — OK. I'll call her tonight.

Matt enters, carrying a bottle of water

Matt Sorry — were you in the middle of something?

Jay No, no — we were just … I keep forgetting the routines.

Matt I never remember them in the first place. Come on, let's eat.

Mandy You'll have to use the machines in the corridor. Those girls are out there again.

Matt Oh God…

Robert enters

Robert Hey, come on, guys, you need to eat something.

Matt There are girls out there again.

Robert So what? You're used to that by now, aren't you?

Matt Yeah, but these ones are bonkers.

Jay Don't worry, Matt, I'll sort them out for you.

Jay heads towards the exit

Robert Try and avoid them, Jay. Take the back exit.

Mandy It's all right, I'll steer him in the right direction.

Mandy exits with Jay

Robert Well?

Matt What?

Robert Are you gonna grab a sandwich or something?

Matt Will you be my bodyguard?

Robert Absolutely. I'll go out first and create a diversion.

Matt They'll probably fancy you more than me.

Robert Oh, God, I hope not.

Matt Be wasted on you, anyway.

Robert Matt!

Matt Well, it would be, wouldn't it? I'm not being horrible, I'm just saying.

Robert Yes, Matt —whatever.

Matt Does Wayland know? About you, I mean?

Robert We avoid the subject. I don't think he likes gays much. Not that it matters — he can't manage without me anyway.

Matt You do make a good team.

Robert Well, it's the perfect combination. I need him to make my mark in the pop business, and he needs me to clear up all his shit.

Matt You enjoying it?

Robert (*sarcastically*) Matt — it's more than I ever dreamed. Now — sandwich or what?

Matt Yeah, OK. But no mad girls.

Robert I know a secret way out, come on. (*He puts his arm affectionately around Matt's shoulders*)

They exit

Black-out

Unit 13

Two teenage girls, Laura and Debbie, camp outside the recording studios. They are dressed head to toe in "Freedom" merchandise. They have a cassette radio at their feet which is playing a "Freedom" recording and a shopping bag containing a bed sheet

Wayland enters on his way to the studio. He stops for a moment and goes back to talk to the girls

Wayland What are you girls doing here? Shouldn't you be in school?

Laura No.

Wayland How do you know the band's recording in there?

Debbie We've got contacts.

Wayland Have you now? You been fans for long?

Laura Since before they were famous. They came to our school.

Debbie Yeah. We were fans before anyone else.

Laura Do you know them? Can you get their autograph?

Wayland No, I just, er — I just work in the building.

Debbie That's a shame. They're really difficult to get to talk to.

Laura Their manager is really strict with them.

Wayland (*enjoying the moment*) Is he?

Debbie Yeah. Apparently he's a real wanker.

Wayland is deflated

Laura We've been to the house where Jay grew up.
Debbie It's in Chelmsford. Manor Drive.
Laura It's easy to tell which one, 'cos people have written "I love you Jay" all over the fence.
Debbie She tried to write it on the front door, but his mum came out.
Laura I was just like that — (*she demonstrates*) when she opened the door. I nearly wrote all over her face.
Debbie We really laughed. Then she told us to sod off.
Laura Which isn't really fair because we'd taken the train and everything.
Debbie Shall we show him the thing?
Laura Go on, then. We sneaked into the hotel where they were staying last night and a maid showed us up to their room.
Wayland Did she now?
Debbie We thought they might've left something behind.
Laura But they hadn't.
Debbie So we nicked a bed sheet.

The girls pull the bed sheet out of the shopping bag and show it to Wayland

Laura One of them actually slept in this!

The girls scream and jump about with excitement. Then they sniff the bed sheet and scream and jump about some more. Wayland decides he has had enough and walks away

Black-out

A video sequence with music shows photos and video footage of the mass hysteria of the fans. It shows crowds of girls, screaming, running, crying, singing; also shots of the boys signing autographs and attending press conferences, and cover shots of teen magazines. One cover declares "'Freedom' Tops the Charts".

UNIT 14

A hotel room shared by three of the boys. It is early in the morning.

A large curtained window dominates the back wall. Matt is asleep in bed. Adam is pacing around the room

Female fans can be heard singing and screaming outside in the street below

Matt (*waking*) What's that noise?

Adam Some of our adoring fans.

Matt How long have you been up?

Adam Hours.

Matt Where's Danny gone?

Adam (*aggressively*) How the hell should I know?

Matt What's up with you?

Adam I'm bored — all right? Bored out of my bloody mind.

Matt How can you be bored? We never have a minute off.

Adam Matt, I spent the whole of March sat on my arse in a recording studio, the whole of April sat on my arse in front of a photographer, and the whole of May sat on my arse answering the questions of idiot reporters. That is not my idea of an interesting life. Every fifteen minutes, the same stupid questions; "So, tell us, Adam, what's your favourite colour?"

Matt And what did you say?

Adam What?

Matt Mine was "Red!". (*He jumps out of bed. He is wearing bright red shorts and matching socks*)

Adam Matt! You're missing the point! Oh, I don't know why I bother.

Matt At least we're always together, the five of us.

Adam Yeah — exactly. We're always together.

Matt What's that supposed to mean?

Adam I'm always surrounded by other people and I don't think I've ever felt so bloody lonely.

Matt (*with hurt*) Maybe you're just bored with all of us.

Adam No. Listen, Matt — you guys are great, just great — I mean that. But I did not choose you to be my friends. Wayland chose you for me. And if I'm going to spend my life locked up with four other people, I'd like some say in who they are.

Matt Why don't you ring your family? That's what I do when I'm feeling down. You should phone your mum and have a good old chat.

Adam I'd have to find her first — and anyway, she wouldn't be interested. Look, I need to score some more stuff, that's the real problem. I've got to get out of here somehow.

Danny enters into the room, carrying a copy of the NME newspaper

Danny You can't. I've tried. They've got us surrounded.

Adam Oh, God! (*He slumps dejectedly on to the floor*)

Danny Have you seen this thing in the NME?

Matt How did you get hold of that?

Danny Calm down — someone left it in the lobby.

Matt Danny, we're not supposed to ——

Danny Matt — it's got a review of the Brighton gig. You wanna hear it or not?

Matt Is it good?

Danny Well the first line gives you a clue — (*reading*) "I've tasted 'Freedom' and it made me nauseous."

Matt Oh, no — I don't want to hear any more.

Danny "Danny Robinson's music is the worst of the teen scene fodder, churned up in the stomach of commercialism and shat out of the arse of Britpop". It's mad — people either worship you or hate your guts.

Matt Come on, Danny, lighten up — your song's at number one, man. Number one!

Danny (*referring to the noise outside*) Yeah — and don't I bloody know it. (*He goes over to the hotel window*)

The crowd outside scream louder when they see Danny

Don't you lot have homes to go to!

Jay and Sean enter

Jay Rise and shine, boys! We're number one and it's time for fun.

Sean Come on, Matt, car leaves in half an hour.

Danny Have you heard this racket?

Sean I went out on the balcony earlier. You should have heard the girls screaming for me — it was classic.

Danny That lot would scream at anything — I bet my arse would get a bigger response than your face did.

Sean Maybe you should try it, then.

Danny I will. (*He goes up to the window, fully separating the curtains and turning his back to the window as he unbuckles his trousers*) Ready, boys? (*He exposes his backside to the crowd below*)

A great cheer and more screams are heard

At this moment Wayland enters

Wayland Danny, get away from there! (*He grabs Danny and pulls him viciously away from the window, then closes the curtains*)

Lots of booing from the crowd is heard

(*Furiously*) What the hell do you think you're doing?

Danny Bit of market research. To find out which has the biggest approval rating, Sean's face or my arse.

Wayland You won't find it so funny when your arse is spread all over the front page of the *Sun* tomorrow.

Danny Wouldn't that be brilliant! "Danny Robinson speaks to the nation".
Wayland You get your act together, boy. I've invested a lot of time and
money in creating a clean image for this band. And I will not have it all
destroyed by some stupid schoolboy stunt.
Danny You know what, Wayland; you sound just like my dad—and I joined
this band to get away from him.
Sean You've got to start acting like a professional, Danny.
Danny I'll start acting like one, when I start getting paid like one.
Sean If you're not happy, why don't you just sod off?
Danny Yeah, you'd love that, wouldn't you?
Sean I'm getting sick of this ... Why don't you ——
Wayland Shut up, Sean — I'll deal with this. (*He goes head on at Danny
and is very vicious*)

Danny retreats

You know exactly how I feel about any lack of discipline within this band.
Don't you ever—ever—pull a stunt like that again! (*To all of them*) Now,
get yourselves ready and meet downstairs. I just got you to number one —
number one for Christ's sake! And this is how you thank me!

*The Lights cross-fade to a spotlight on Wayland. He remains in the spotlight
as the scene changes*

Unseen, the boys exit

Wayland steps forward

Unseen, Mandy and Robert enter

UNIT 15

The spotlight opens out to reveal Robert and Mandy

Mandy I'm sure it won't happen again.
Robert The tour's nearly over. It's just the pressure.
Wayland I'm not risking another stunt like that. Not when we're right up
there at the top. You think it's pressure?
Robert Of course it is.
Wayland Fine. Let's give them a bit of relief—let them off-load a bit of their
stress.
Mandy How exactly?
Wayland Sex. We'll bend the rules for a couple of nights, let them have girls
up to their rooms.

Robert What girls?

Wayland There are dozens out there right now. Just take a few aside and see if they're interested.

Robert And you're sure about this?

Wayland They'll have to sign something first — we don't want any kiss 'n' tell stuff later. And, Robert, you make sure they're over sixteen. Check ID's and everything. I don't care how cute they are. If they can't prove their age, they can't screw the band.

Robert What about Matt?

Wayland What about him?

Robert Well you might want to leave him out of this.

Wayland Why?

Robert I don't think he's into girls.

Wayland What are you talking about?

Robert I'm telling you — I really don't think — he'll be interested.

Wayland What are you saying to me? Is Matt ...?

Robert I think so.

Wayland Oh shit! That's all I need! Now you two listen to me — if Matt has any sexual preferences other than those I *want* him to have, he can damn well keep them to himself. Do you understand?

Mandy Don't be ridiculous, you can't ——

Wayland Can't what? What can't I do?

Mandy You can't control everything. You can't decide who they are.

Wayland Don't tell me my job, Mandy — just get on with your own. Now, Robert — find out about Matt for sure. I want to know exactly what we're dealing with here. And just to be safe, we'll put out a story that Matt's a virgin — and a Catholic; that one always works. For now, send him up a girl to his room anyway; hopefully he will screw her, and if not — they can always exchange recipes.

Mandy You're being completely insensitive.

Wayland I am their manager, not their father.

Mandy Maybe at times like these, you need to be a bit of both.

Wayland What? Oh, shut up.

Mandy Don't tell me to shut up!

Wayland All right — calm down. We'll discuss this later tonight.

Mandy No, we won't.

Mandy exits

Wayland (*calling off*) Mandy —do we have time for this? I mean — isn't there enough on my bloody plate?

Robert Just leave her.

Wayland If she wasn't such a damn good choreographer, I'd tell her to pack her bags. (*Calling off*) Mandy!

Robert She's gone.

Wayland I can see that — thank you! Christ, it's all going crap tonight. Shit!

Robert Wayland, look — about this thing with the girls ——

Wayland We're still doing it! It's no good just controlling their careers, Robert. You have to control the whole thing. That's the deal. Their social lives, their emotions, sex lives, the lot. That's how you keep them where you want them. That's how the money's made. So — we fix them up with some girls — and that means Matt as well. Let's at least give him a chance ... Send him a butch one — with hair on her arms.

Robert And you want me to tell them before the gig?

Wayland Oh, yes. It'll give the concert a real kick when they know what's coming afterwards. (*He has a sudden thought*) And we need condoms! Big packs of them.

Robert stares at Wayland, now very uncertain about this

Don't look at me like that. I've given these boys the world, haven't I?

Black-out

Unit 16

A concert sequence. This is the most spectacular so far

Adam sings the lead on the first number

Song No. 6 — What Good Is a Heart

The second number is filmed live by a camera operator (Robert on this occasion) and relayed on to the video screen. The backing dancers feature in this number, with the option of Mandy dancing with them

Sean sings lead vocal

Song No. 7 — Turn It Into Something Good*

In the European tour of BoyBand, this number was replaced by the song called **Driving Me Crazy. Please see page vii for further details.*

Interval

ACT II

Unit 17

Unseen as yet, is the setting for the changing-rooms backstage

A spectacular concert sequence takes place. The opening number features the backing dancers. The band are wearing bright, funky costumes. Jay sings lead vocal

Song No. 8 — Have Fun Go Mad

When the number has finished, Sean steps forward

During the following, a keyboard or a piano is brought onto the stage

Sean (*speaking to the crowd*) I've had a brilliant night and you've been an amazing crowd. Birmingham — I love ya!

Screams from the crowd are heard

I'm gonna take the mood down a little bit now — 'cos it's time for me, and my guys, to say goodbye.

Danny is in disbelief at the speech. Sean removes his jacket and passes it to Danny to hold. Danny is seething with anger, but bottles it up for a moment. Sean starts the next song. It is a solo number with brief backing harmony. Sean accompanies himself on keyboards (either live or miming). Alternatively, Danny accompanies Sean on the keyboards

Song No. 9 — Gentle Love

Sean takes the applause

The band wave their way off-stage

The Lights cross-fade to the changing-room backstage. A reporter and photographer are waiting for them in the room. The roar of the screaming crowd can be heard in the background throughout the scene

The boys enter, led by Danny. They carry their microphones

Danny You two — out.
Reporter We've arranged an interview — it's all been approved.
Danny I don't care — I want you out of here — now.

The reporter and photographer exit

Danny rounds on Sean as soon as the reporter and photographer exit

Danny I'm not going back on stage with him.
Adam Danny, we have to — listen to them screaming out there.
Danny "It's time for me, and my guys, to say goodbye!" What the hell is that all about?
Sean What's the problem?
Danny Had you forgotten — we're a group, we're not just there to make you look good.
Sean Danny — I don't have the energy for this.
Danny Oh, well excuse me. You must be tired after your solo performance. Us poor bastards in the background have loads of energy left.
Sean Why don't you calm down and get changed?
Danny You stood there taking the applause like we didn't even exist.
Sean Oh, that's what it is — I offended your ego.
Danny *My* ego?
Sean Just shut it, will you. Get on with your job, like the rest of us.
Danny And what is my job exactly — second harmony with "Sean and the Seanettes"?
Jay Danny, leave it now.
Danny No — we need to talk about this.
Jay Not now we don't. People can hear.
Danny I don't care. (*To Sean*) You made us look like nothing with your speeches out there tonight. It was like you owned us, like you were doing us a favour.
Sean Look — every band needs a front man. Just you remember it was me that brought you into this group in the first place ...
Danny Wayland brought me in ——
Sean Wayland and me. I approved you.
Danny I can't believe this — you trying to tell me that you're my boss, that I have to be grateful to a dickhead like you.
Sean If you don't shut it ——
Danny You're nothing but an arrogant arsehole.

Sean throws a punch at Danny and they both start fighting. The others try to break them up. Lots of commotion

At this moment, the reporter and photographer burst back into the room

The photographer takes a series of flash pictures of the fight

Adam and Matt bundle the journalist and photographer out of the room

Jay separates Sean and Danny

Jay That's enough! Are you happy now? That's going to be all over the papers by the morning.
Matt Wayland's gonna go ballistic.
Jay Look — you don't have to like each other, or even talk to each other. But can you at least avoid punching each other's lights out? We're back in the studio tomorrow — just a few more sessions and the album's finished. So let's try not to kill each other before then. Now get back out there — all of you — now!

The boys start to make their way to the exit. Sean turns back to confront Jay

Sean Who put you in charge all of a sudden?

Jay slaps a microphone into Sean's hand and pushes him c

Jay and the others exit

A spotlight comes up on Sean as though he has just walked on to the concert stage. Further lights are added during the following

The other boys enter

The crowd roars its approval

(*Addressing the audience*) Thanks very much. You've been a fantastic crowd. We've got one more song for you tonight. You'll remember this one from last summer — this was our first ever number one. (*He sings lead vocal*)

During the song, we notice aggressive looks being exchanged between Sean and Danny, though they keep up a reasonably professional front before the audience

Song No. 10 — All This and Heaven Too

Black-out

UNIT 18

Unseen as yet is the setting for Wayland's office. There are piles of newspapers on the desk

The following dialogue is shown as a video sequence. It shows a late night news programme looking at the next day's newspapers. As the presenter discusses the papers, we see shots of the covers of the "Daily Mail" and the "Mirror", each sporting a photo of the Sean and Danny fight

Presenter And before we go, a look at tomorrow's papers. And they're dominated by dramatic photographs of a backstage fight between members of the pop group "Freedom". These were taken in Birmingham, the final date on a sell-out national tour. The band has enjoyed a meteoric rise to fame since they first emerged two years ago and are currently recording their third album. But the papers tomorrow have clearly decided that the days of the band are numbered. The *Mail* has "Freedom concert packs a punch" and in the *Mirror* it's "Fists fly for Freedom's final freefall — bye bye boy band". Well, it's "bye bye" from us as well because that's all we have time for. Good-night.

The video sequence ends. The Lights rise on Wayland's office

Mandy, Robert and Wayland sift through the piles of newspapers

Wayland Well, this is just great. A run of brilliant concerts, two hit albums, and what's on the front page? Sean and Danny thumping each other.
Robert We've had to deal with bad publicity before.
Wayland Not like this. This is different. They can slag off the music and the hype as much as they like, because those fans don't give a damn what they write about that. But when they find out the boys they dream about hate each other's guts — that's it, the dream is over. Any boy band has a limited shelf life. Once the illusion is shattered, those fans will just move on. Straight to the next bunch of boys that they *can* believe in.
Robert So, what do we do about it?
Wayland You just keep them happy until the Wembley concerts. I'm gonna make a fortune on those gigs and I'm not having anyone getting between me and that pay-day. Once Wembley's over, if they insist on self-destructing, fine. We'll just dump them.
Mandy Dump them!?
Wayland I'm not going down with a sinking ship. Not this time. I've got my reputation to think of now.
Mandy What about the third album?

Wayland What about it? I've got all the advances. And they're non-returnable, I made sure of that.

Robert But when's it going to be released?

Wayland My guess is never. It won't be worth it. Who's going to buy an album from a band that's torn itself apart?

Mandy So after all their sweat and hard work, those boys will come out of this with absolutely nothing?

Wayland They've got thousands of girls throwing themselves at their feet — what more does a kid want? Look if they want to screw up their careers, that's up to them.

Robert Hang on, Wayland. You owe them more than that.

Wayland I owe them nothing! This is a business. And it's a business that's growing fast. I'm taking my money and my reputation and I'm going to invest them in new projects — big things, Robert. If you want to be part of that, you better learn to play my way. Now — are you on board or not?

A pause

Robert Well, if we're going to keep them together till Wembley, someone needs to talk to Danny.

Wayland Exactly.

Robert And it's the Brit Awards tonight. Wait till Sean and Danny start thumping each other on live television.

Wayland You leave that to me. I'm going down to the studio right now. It's time to put Mr Danny Robinson back in his box.

Wayland exits

Mandy You can't let him do this.

Robert I don't have a choice. If he decides to dump them, no-one can stop him.

Mandy And you're fine with that?

Robert No, of course I'm not.

Mandy Well, you didn't exactly stand up to him. And you should have done, you're the one guy he listens to.

Robert I can only push things so far. I don't want to lose my job.

Mandy Robert, haven't you been listening? If he does this to the band, it's all over — there is no job.

Robert Maybe not with these guys, but with other bands, with other ——

Mandy You really think he's gonna manage to pull off something like this again? He's a used car dealer that just got lucky, that's all.

Robert Well, I'll be there to run the show with him in the future, it'll be different.

Mandy Robert, if you think you've got the talent to do that — then do it on your own. You've made a name for yourself now, what the bloody hell do you need him for? (*She pauses*) Just think about the boys for a minute. They will come out with no money; nothing. Doesn't that bother you? Jay, Adam — Matt will come out with nothing.

Robert OK, so — it's not a situation we're happy with. But what can we ——

Mandy The boys have some power this time.

Robert Mandy ——

Mandy They do. Just hear me out. Look, you know how badly Wayland needs Wembley. He's put all the earnings from the last two years into promotion and the clearing of his debts. Wembley is the first time he'll ever make serious money. It's totally sold out. This is the moment at which he cashes in and walks away a wealthy man.

Robert Well?

Mandy What if the band didn't show? What if they just didn't turn up?

Robert He's insured. Non-appearance, cancellation; he's covered for all of it.

Mandy Wrong — he never wrote the cheque. He couldn't bring himself to pay out all that money. A cancellation would mean he wouldn't get a single penny.

Robert And Wembley would sue him. My God, they'd skin him alive.

Mandy Exactly. Wayland would be finished. And all it needs is for someone to tell that to the boys.

Mandy prepares to go

Robert Mandy— look, there is no way that I'm going to just sit here while you tell those guys how to destroy their own manager.

Mandy And how do you think you're gonna stop me?

Robert I'm gonna tell them myself. I'll be at the studio.

Robert exits

UNIT 19

The recording studio

Music

The band are putting down vocal tracks. Sean sings lead vocal on the number while the others sing the harmonies. After a few bars, Danny signals to cut the track off. The music stops. Sean removes his headphones

Sean What's the problem?

Danny I don't think this is working.

Sean What do you mean?

Danny The song's just not right. It needs a different feel to it.

Sean Sounded all right to me.

Danny Look, I think we should try it again — with Adam singing the lead.

Sean No. We'll leave it exactly as it is. I want to do this one.

Danny Sean, why do we have to do this every time? I wrote the damn song, so if I say that Adam's voice would sound better, we should at least try it.

Sean We haven't got time to waste on stupid experiments. It sounds fine, so let's just leave it.

Danny I told you — I want Adam on this!

Adam I'm going out for a smoke.

Jay What?

Adam Well I've seen this show before, and I know how it ends.

Jay Adam, sit down.

Adam No, I'm going for a ——

Jay Don't we have enough to deal with, without you lighting up a joint every ten minutes. You've been told a hundred times not to do it.

Adam I don't care what Wayland ——

Jay I don't care either. I'm telling you *I* don't like it. All right? *Me*. Every time any kind of crisis happens, you get on the first bus to Nirvana.

Adam Don't start on me — it's those two that are at each other's throats.

Danny (*to Adam*) I was trying to stick up for you.

Adam It's not worth the aggravation.

Danny It is.

Adam Not to me.

Danny I'm sick of him ignoring everything I've got to say.

Adam Well you're ignoring everything I've got to ——

Sean That's because everything you say is crap.

Danny Do you actually *want* me to hit you?

Wayland enters

Wayland All right, all right — what the bloody hell is it this time?

Sean Danny's picking fights as usual. He's trying to drop me from the song 'cos he knows it'll wind me up.

Danny You're pathetic ——

Wayland All right, that's enough! Danny, stay here. Everyone else, get out.

The boys make their way to the exit

(*Grabbing Adam as he passes*) And if I catch you trying to light one up out there, I'll ram it all the way down your bloody throat. *Comprendez*?

The boys exit

Wayland and Danny are alone

This stops right now, Danny.

Danny What?

Wayland You've had it in for Sean for months and now it's gonna stop.

Danny It's got nothing to do with you.

Wayland What?

Danny We'll sort it out for ourselves. We're not kids any more. You may have control of the business side, but we'll handle everything else.

Wayland Don't think you can shut me out, you stupid little prick. Two years ago you were stacking shelves in Tesco's and you'd still be there if it wasn't for me.

Danny I would've made it in the end, Wayland, with or without you.

Wayland In your dreams, pal. You just got lucky I found you.

Danny Lucky?

Wayland Yes — lucky. If it wasn't you five, it would've been five others, any five out of a thousand. And don't think you're the only songwriter that's ever walked through my door. There's dozens in my files every bit as good as you — just remember that. The only reason that someone like you is famous is because of me — the boss, the suit — my hard work, my drive, my skill. All you do is get the adoration.

Danny And one pound twenty an hour, don't forget that — I'm saving up for an ice-cream!

Wayland Don't try and be funny.

Danny You may not have noticed, but people up and down the country are singing my songs.

Wayland People sing songs from tampon commercials. Adverts, game shows — any crappy song from the radio, as long as it's played often enough. Half the songs people whistle to are ones they don't even like! It's not about songs, son — it's about marketing, image and airplay. You're just a product. A piece of merchandise that's been created, developed and packaged by me.

Danny See, I look at it differently. I think we're the ones that made *you*.

Wayland Oh, shut up — you don't know what you're talking about.

Danny Every band you touched before was a total washout. Wasn't it? And the funny thing is, if you left the band, some other manager would step in and we'd carry on just as before, no-one would even notice. But if I left, you and your bank manager would be well stuffed!

Wayland Now you listen to me. This is your final warning. You get back in line or ——

Danny Or what? What will you do? Sack me? What would happen to your precious little product then?

Wayland (*strongly*) Don't push it with me, Danny.
Danny I want Adam to sing lead on that song. And if he doesn't, I walk.
  Comprendez?

Danny walks off-stage

Black-out

UNIT 20

A canteen in the recording studio

Matt is alone, having a drink. He is looking a bit glum

Robert enters

Robert Matt, where are the others? I need to talk to you all.
Matt They're outside getting some air. Danny's still in the studio.
Robert With Wayland?
Matt Yeah.
Robert Damn.
Matt What's wrong?
Robert Nothing, there's just something I need to tell you.
Matt Well, why don't you tell me?
Robert No — I want to tell all of you together. (*He notices Matt*) You OK?
Matt Not really. It's just not much fun these days, is it? Everyone seems to
  be losing it. Sean and Danny fight all the time, Jay always has to keep them
  apart. And all Adam cares about is where the next spliff is coming from.
  No-one smiles any more — not even me.
Robert Well, it's a serious business.
Matt Shouldn't be though, should it? Not at our age. The biggest crisis my
  mates at home have to deal with is whether to have a Fosters or a Heineken.
  Are you gonna come to the awards tonight?
Robert Are you kidding? "Freedom" win Best British Group at the Brit
  Awards? Of course I'll be there.
Matt Oh, great. You can keep me company. It's easier to cope with all that
  bickering when you're around. Who knows, we might even enjoy ourselves.
Robert Matt, I'll be working. It's not exactly going to be a romantic evening
  out.
Matt "Romantic"? What do you mean?
Robert I mean — it won't be particularly pleasant.
Matt No, I know what you meant. You think I'm ... You do, don't you?
Robert Matt. I know all the teen mags have been told you're a virgin but give
  me a little credit.

Matt I am a virgin.

Robert Yeah, right.

Matt (*sharply*) Look, Robert, just because you're gay, it doesn't mean everyone else is. (*He stands*) I think I better go.

Robert Matt ... Look, I'm sorry, mate, I didn't mean anything by it — I was ——

Matt Robert, I don't ... Just — leave me alone.

Robert (*backing away*) All right, all right — I'm sorry.

Robert exits

Matt is left standing there for a moment, confused. The Lights slowly fade, leaving him dimly lit in a spotlight

The following dialogue is a video sequence. It shows the presenter introducing the band at the Brit Awards. During the following, Matt moves into position

Unseen, the other boys enter and get into their opening position, seated around Matt. They are wearing matching suits

Brit Award Host Now on the Brit Awards, a band who are hotly tipped tonight to win Best British Group. They've had seven hit singles, two number one albums and they always put on a good show — particularly backstage. Will you please welcome — "Freedom".

The video link ends and the light on Matt opens out to reveal all of the boys in their opening positions for the next number

Matt sings lead vocal

Song No. 11 — Every Day Hurts

Black-out

Unit 21

The backstage area of the "Brit Awards" venue

There is a payphone. Jay is in the middle of a call

Jay (*into the telephone*) Did he recognize me? ... Yeah? ... Brilliant. ... No, we're gonna get the award in a minute. When are you gonna ... ?

The other boys enter. Adam is first

(*Into the telephone*) I can't talk now — gotta go. (*He hangs up*)

Adam notices

Wayland and Robert enter

Wayland Now, I want just Danny and Sean to collect the award — show the world at large what great mates you are — OK? And remember to look surprised, because we're not supposed to know we've won it. So, Adam, Matt and Jay, go and get changed, Ike and Tina Turner — follow me.

Wayland leads Danny and Sean off. Danny goose-steps behind Wayland with a Nazi salute. Adam and Jay exit

Robert immediately approaches Matt

Robert Matt, please — let me apologize ——
Matt It's all right.
Robert It's not all right, I just … I feel so stupid.
Matt Robert, it's not you — it's me. I spend my whole life with people telling me what to do and what to say, and who to be. I don't even get to think for myself. I've so lost track of everything — I don't even know what I want — there hasn't been the time. Oh, this is such a mess.
Robert Hey — look, let's just be friends, all right? Why don't we just take some time and go out for a proper talk?
Matt You gonna buy me dinner?
Robert You'll be lucky.

A short pause

Matt How am I gonna survive all this?
Robert Just keep smiling.

Matt gives Robert a hug. There is a moment between them. They kiss

Wayland enters

Wayland (*greatly shocked at seeing Matt and Robert in their clinch*) What the bloody hell are you doing!?!
Matt (*breaking apart*) Nothing.
Wayland Nothing!? It didn't look like nothing to me!
Robert Let's just forget about this, Wayland. We can talk about it later.
Wayland Oh yes, we'll just forget about it. After all, it's no big deal is it —

hundreds of thousands of pounds riding on a straight, wholesome image, and the gay PA is trying to screw the lot of them in public!

Robert I think you should calm down ——

Wayland Shut up! I knew it, I knew this would happen — from the moment you first talked about Matt. But I thought you were a professional, I thought we were a team! But you just can't keep your hands off, can you?

Robert This is none of your business.

Wayland Everything is my business. Are you two completely thick? There are reporters crawling all over this building. Matt — are you prepared to lose your entire career over him?

Robert Don't be stupid ——

Wayland Oh yeah, that's me, always the stupid one. Get out, Robert, you're fired.

Robert What!?

Wayland You heard; fired!

Robert Oh, well that's a really adult way to deal with this ——

Wayland Just get out!

Robert Fine. You don't need me around — you're dumping the guys after Wembley, anyway.

Wayland Will you piss off before I have security throw you out!

Robert exits

Matt What's he talking about?

Wayland Go to the dressing-room and get changed — now!

Wayland exits

Matt is left behind, shaken

After a few moments, Danny enters laughing to himself and clutching the Brit Awards trophy

Danny Did you see that? Brilliant. I just made Sean look a complete prat on prime-time television, it was classic. Matt! Did you see it?

Matt No!

Danny (*realizing immediately*) All right — what's happened this time?

Matt Wayland just sacked Robert.

Danny Why?

Matt Robert's gay, Danny.

Danny Is he? What a surprise! What are you gonna tell me next, that the Pope's Catholic? That in the woods, big brown bears have a good sh ——

Matt All right, all right — I get the picture.

Danny So, come on — what's this all about?

Matt doesn't respond

Danny Oh, don't get all shy on me, Matt, I haven't got the patience.

Matt Well, me and Robert ... We were thinking of — seeing each other.

Danny And is that why Wayland fired him?

Matt Yeah.

Danny What a prat!... Well you can still see Robert, can't you? It'll be easier now. It can be out in the open.

Matt Oh come on, Danny, be realistic. It's not ideal is it. I mean, there I am on the bedroom walls of a thousand teenage girls — and all the time, I'm more interested in their brothers! If news of something like that got out, we'd be finished.

Danny Well maybe that'd be a good thing. We're all hanging on in there for our pot of gold, but it's not worth it if you can't have a life, is it?

Matt I'm not bothered about the money.

Danny Well then, let's tell Wayland to stuff it. I've been dreaming of doing that for weeks.

Matt Yeah, but what happens then? What do I do afterwards? I mean, I can't really do anything, can I. I can't stand up there on my own; I can't play any instruments; I can't write material.

Danny You've started writing your own songs.

Matt Oh they're crap, Danny, really bad — they're even worse than Sean's. I can't do it. And I can't go back to working in a shop, everyone would just laugh at me. See, if the band finishes, then I'm finished too. And I'm not ready for that.

Danny So you don't want to get out and I don't want to stay in. It's mad.

Matt This whole thing is mad. There's nothing normal about any of it. Even when I go home, there's all these weirdos hanging around — it's like I'm some kind of magnet for nutters. There's this woman who turns up at my mum and dad's house every Sunday. She brings her whole family with her. They sit in the drive, and they have a picnic! On the drive, every Sunday. I don't understand any of it. I'm gonna crack up, Danny, I really am. It's just — it's getting too much.

Danny So what are we gonna do about it?

Matt We have to see it through to Wembley, don't we? We owe it to the fans.

Danny Yeah. And once we've played Wembley, we'll finally get that third album.

Matt I don't know, Danny.

Danny Eh?

Matt There was something Robert said as he was leaving.

Danny What?
Matt That, after Wembley — Wayland's gonna dump us. He wouldn't do
that, would he?

A slight pause

Danny You got Robert's number?

Black-out

UNIT 22

*Unseen as yet is the setting for the Wembley stage. Bits of rigging line the
stage*

The following dialogue shows as a video sequence. It is MTV news

MTV Presenter And finally — mega boy band "Freedom" are preparing
for their first ever concert at Wembley. The shows were sold out long
before all the recent media coverage surrounding the disagreements within
the band and many fans believe that this could be their last chance to see
the boys perform. And still there is no release date for the eagerly awaited
third album — adding to speculation that the days of "Freedom" really are
numbered. Is this the end for the "Freedom" boys? Watch this space.

The Lights come up on the Wembley stage

*Adam is alone on the stage, sitting on a piece of the rig. Looking round to
check that nobody is watching him, he takes out a pouch from his pocket that
contains a small mirror and a tiny tin of cocaine. He prepares the powder
quickly and sniffs it*

  Jay enters

*Adam is taken by surprise and quickly hides the pouch, but drops the tin. Jay
watches it fall to the floor. Adam goes to pick it up*

Jay Just leave it, Adam.
Adam What?
Jay I'm surprised you even bother to try to hide all this from us these days.
We all know what's going on.
Adam Can I just have some privacy? I wanted a moment alone.

Adam picks up the tin and puts it in his pocket

Jay Yeah, right — I know what you wanted. What is it this time?
Adam Jay — just sod off.

Jay crosses to Adam and holds out his hand. Adam ignores him. After a moment, Jay just grabs the items from Adam's pocket. Adam hardly resists. Jay quickly examines the items

Jay (*angrily*) You have got to be kidding! You want me to have to go over this again?
Adam No, I just want to be left alone.
Jay Well, I'm not gonna do that. Not while you're doing stuff like this. You're a bloody idiot.
Adam I don't have to take this from you — you're not my father.
Jay No, and thank Christ for that! I despair of all you guys, I really do.
Adam Jay — just get off your high horse for five minutes will you. You're not so perfect yourself.
Jay What?
Adam Every time you get near a phone, you're chatting some girl up.
Jay That's Shelley — she's just a friend.
Adam Yeah, right. Tell you what, you screw her and I'll take that — OK?
Jay No way. (*He empties the tin onto the floor*)
Adam Jay! I haven't even paid for that yet.
Jay Who was it? One of the roadies sell it to you?
Adam Does it matter?
Jay Yes, Adam. Yes, it does — here in the real world. You're a bloody fool, mate, you don't even know how those drugs are affecting you.
Adam They help me relax.
Jay If I whack you on the head with a brick, that'll help you relax too — so don't tempt me.
Adam Why are you always trying to hold everything together? Why don't you just kick it to bits like the rest of us?
Jay Because I can't afford to.
Adam Money isn't everything, Jay.
Jay I don't need it for me. Oh, you wouldn't understand.
Adam Me? No, of course not, I don't understand anything.
Jay You should open your eyes sometimes, Adam. You're not the only one with problems, you know.

Sean, Matt and Danny enter

Sean OK, guys, they want us to run the number again so that the lighting designer can have a look at it.
Adam What, the whole thing?

Sean Yes, all of it. And remember, guys — this is Wembley. So let's give it loads of energy.

They take their opening positions for the number

The backing track for the number "Better Be Good" starts playing

Sean gives the routine plenty of energy, but the others present a tired, totally minimal version of the choreography. After a while, Danny becomes bored and starts mimicking and mocking Sean's style and gestures. And when the choreography puts them near to each other, he gets deliberately too close in order to wind Sean up. Eventually, Sean explodes and shoves Danny away from him

Danny Don't shove me about—you keep your bloody hands away from me!
Sean You were out of position.
Danny You mean I was blocking the audience's view of your ugly face.
Sean Don't get arsey with me just because you forgot the routine.

The backing track is taken off

Danny Sod the routine.
Sean This is Wembley, Danny, not one of them girls' schools — it's got to be right. I'm not gonna look a prat because of you.
Danny You don't need any help to look a prat, Sean. You were born one.

Danny and Sean break into a serious fight

Wayland charges on to the stage

Adam and Matt pull Sean out of the fight and restrain him. Jay grabs Danny

Wayland All right, that's enough! Danny, get off the stage.
Danny (*dangerously*) You what?
Jay (*to Wayland*) I'll deal with this.
Wayland Like hell you will! Danny — off the stage, now.
Danny You don't control me, Wayland. You can shove it.
Sean Fire him! Why don't you fire him?
Wayland Shut up, Sean!
Sean We'll work around him, use my songs — just fire him.
Danny He can't.
Sean You watch him!
Danny He can't — he needs me too much. I am the product, aren't I,

Wayland? If anyone gets the sack round here, it should be you. You're the useless one.

Wayland You little scumbag.

Danny How does it feel to be losing your grip, eh, Wayland? How does it feel to lose control?

Wayland loses his temper completely and goes for Danny. He throws a punch, which Danny ducks. Danny thumps him in the face. With a yelp, Wayland falls to the floor

Danny That's it! I'm out of here. (*He marches towards the exit*)

Jay stops Danny

Jay Don't blow it, Danny. Don't chuck it away. Just a few more weeks and we'll all start making money.

Danny It's not going to happen, Jay. He's dumping us after Wembley — no third album, no payback, nothing. Ask Robert. Or better still, ask him.

Danny exits

The other boys gather over Wayland

Jay What did he mean you're going to dump us after ——

Wayland Just get out of here! Go! All of you! Take the weekend off and leave me alone. But I want you back here Monday morning — nine o'clock sharp.

They all exit leaving Sean and Wayland

Sean You all right, boss?

Wayland Oh yeah, never been better!

Sean You know — I don't think this is bad news at all.

Wayland (*with disbelief*) What?

Sean This gives us the perfect chance to launch my solo career. It's always been the plan, hasn't it? Come out of "Freedom" as a solo artist and cross over into a more adult market. This gives us a golden opportunity.

Wayland struggles to his feet

Wayland Sean — There's an old saying; "You can't make chicken soup out of chicken shit". You understand?

Sean doesn't

Your song-writing — it's crap. You'd never make it solo in a million years.
Besides which, you need a very special personality for that, and an ego the
size of the Titanic isn't the only requirement.

Sean But you always said ——

Wayland Forget what I said — what people want now is "Freedom". And
"Freedom" includes Danny Robinson. If you want any kind of future in this
business, Sean, there's only one thing you can do — get Danny back.

Black-out

UNIT 23

Unseen as yet is the setting for Wayland's office

*The following dialogue shows as a video sequence. It is television breakfast
news*

TV Presenter And reports are coming in of extraordinary events, involving
"Freedom" songwriter, Danny Robinson. The Dannster has been spotted
in literally dozens of London pubs and clubs, drinking very heavily and
posing in his drunken state for photographers. This will come as a great
shock to the many teenage fans who have grown up with "Freedom"'s
clean and wholesome image. Dan-boy's drunken spree has led to speculation
that he has walked out on "Freedom" and that the band may now split
completely. One thing is for certain — it's hard to keep these guys out of
the headlines.

*To music "Have Fun Go Mad", we see a series of Polaroid snapshots of
Danny, very drunk, with arms around girls, guzzling alcohol, smoking
cigarettes, shouting abuse, etc. The final image is the front page of the* Sun
*newspaper. The headline says "Danny Robinson speaks to the nation" and
the picture is a photo of his backside*

*The Lights rise on Wayland's office. Wayland is sat dejectedly at his desk
looking at the "Sun"'s cover story. Mandy looks over Wayland's shoulder*

Wayland Well, we finally made the front page of the *Sun*. That little shithead
is gonna ruin me. We'll have to pull Wembley, the bastards will sue me —
and I'll lose the lot.

Mandy If you'd paid him properly in the first place, this wouldn't be
happening.

Wayland And why should I pay him more when I'm the one taking all the
risk?

Mandy Because he's got something you'll never have.

Wayland And what's that?

Mandy Talent. If it wasn't for their talent, this band would have sunk without trace years ago.

Wayland But without me, there would have been no band in the first place.

The phone rings. Wayland picks up the reciever

(*Into the phone*) No comment, piss off. (*He puts the receiver down*) If you think I'm such a no-talent shit, why are you still here?

Mandy For the band, Wayland — for those boys. They're the only reason I've ever been here.

Wayland You used me.

Mandy No, I didn't. We had our moment. But it finished. And whatever was going on, I did my job — and I did it well. I just never expected you to become such a bastard.

Wayland Look, OK, so I'm a bastard. Fine. But even if I did screw up here and there — I do not deserve this! Oh, Christ, Mandy — what am I gonna do?

Mandy You'll have to talk to Danny.

Wayland I've got to find him first.

Mandy Have you tried Jay?

Wayland I've tried all of them. None of the bastards showed up for work this morning — they've all buggered off somewhere.

The phone rings again. Wayland answers it

(*Into the phone*) Look, whoever you are, will you please just piss off. ... Danny? ... No, no, I didn't mean you. Where are you? ... Which meeting room? ... Yes — yes I will be there. (*He puts the receiver down*) He's upstairs. (*He puts his jacket on*)

Wayland heads out of the office setting but remains on stage. Lights follow Wayland around the stage as the scene is set for the meeting room. As he walks, we hear the final bars of "Have Fun Go Mad"

During the scene change, Mandy exits. Danny, Matt, Adam and Jay enter unseen

The Lights come up on the meeting room. Adam, Jay and Matt are sitting in a line of three chairs. Danny is at the far end of the line. His chair is further DS and facing across. An empty chair waits for Wayland at the opposite end, next to Matt and opposite Danny

The final notes of the music play out as Wayland enters the meeting room setting

Well, this is a nice little conspiracy, isn't it?

Danny We've got a proposition for you. Now you can take it or leave it but it's not up for negotiation. I've got a bloody awful hangover and I'm not in the mood for arguments.

Wayland Proposition?

Danny gestures for Wayland to sit in the empty seat

Danny See, once I sobered up, we all got together and had a good chat. We've never really done that before, you always seemed to get in the way.

Wayland Yeah, yeah — get on with it.

Danny I'm prepared to come back, and the boys are prepared to stick together — but on the following conditions: first, we tear up the contract. From this moment on, anything this band makes, we split the profits six ways.

Wayland After Wembley.

Danny Including Wembley.

Wayland Forget it. (*He stands and starts to walk out*)

Danny Alternatively, we can just cancel the gigs and sit back while Wembley sue you for breach of contract.

Wayland If you don't do Wembley, you're in breach of *my* contract.

Danny Oh, yeah — we'd have to give you back our hundred pound a week.

A slight pause

Wayland And if I agree to this, you're back in and you do the gig?

Danny Jay?

Jay gestures to the empty chair. Wayland sits again

Jay Also, there's this girl I'm gonna be seeing. And you have to be cool with that. I must be able to have a private life.

Wayland Oh, must you now?

Jay OK?

Wayland Yes, whatever. I'm very happy for you. Don't get her pregnant ——

Jay And I've got a kid.

Wayland What!

Jay A boy — called Jack.

Wayland When the bloody hell did you get time to do that?

Jay He's two years old.
Wayland Did you lot know about this?
Adam Nobody knew about it — not till yesterday.

A slight pause

Wayland Fine. What the hell. Try and avoid having any more; get yourself
another hobby. (*He stands*) OK — are we done?
Danny Matt?

Infuriated, Wayland sits again

Matt I want to be able to see who I want, when I want. I want to just be myself.
And I want you to give Robert his job back.
Wayland You have got to be joking — absolutely not!

The boys stand up and start to leave. Wayland leaps to his feet

(*Panicking*) All right, all right — wait a second —

The boys pause

He can base in a separate office. If that's what he wants.

*Matt nods his agreement. They all resume their seats. Wayland remains
standing*

Well? Is that it? Can we get back to work now? I mean, that's if there's still
something worth working for. You have to realize that you're creating a
serious marketing problem here. I gave the world a whiter than white,
squeaky clean boy band. And you're giving me back; an alcoholic, a drug
addict, a dad — and a friend of Dorothy! I mean — I'm just making a point
here. Screw around with the formula and you're in trouble.
Danny Oh, I dunno — I think our fans might quite enjoy a change to the
formula.
Wayland You can't be serious.
Danny Oh, relax — I'm no alcoholic. I just crammed two years of drinking
into one weekend.
Adam And I've agreed to give up the drugs — permanently.
Matt And I don't know any girls called Dorothy …
Danny So — if we're all agreed, we can get on and sign the new contract.
Wayland Contract? Who said anything about a contract?
Danny Well it's important to get these things in writing, isn't it, Wayland?

Not that we don't trust you or anything.

Wayland Whose idea was all this? None of you lot have got the experience to work all this out. Come on, who's behind it all, who is it?

Sean enters, carrying a clipboard with a contract attached

Sean Sorry I'm late, I was just running off your copy. (*To Wayland*) Well, you did want me to get Danny back.

Wayland You, Sean, are a treacherous piece of ——

Sean Chicken shit? (*He gives Wayland the contract*) It's all very clear. Robert helped with the small print. Everything's in there that Danny's talked about. There's even a release date for the third album.

Wayland But you and Danny hate each other's guts. Or am I supposed to believe that suddenly everything between you is sweetness and light?

Danny No. I still think he's an arrogant slime-ball.

Sean And I still think he's a loud-mouthed idiot. But that doesn't mean we can't work together.

Danny As long as we don't have to live together.

Wayland (*shaking his head*) I don't believe this.

Adam And there's one other thing — we're changing the format for the concert. We're gonna use it to tell the fans the whole story about us, from the beginning. The truth.

Wayland Are you crazy? We've spent two years carefully covering up the truth and now you want to blow it all apart!? You think anyone's going to be interested in you once they find out what you're really like?

Matt That's what we want to find out.

Danny From now on, all decisions regarding our professional and our social lives will be made by us.

Jay If you can't live with that ——

Adam If you don't trust us ——

Matt If you can't respect us ——

Sean Now is the time to walk.

Danny (*mimicking Wayland's original speech and gestures from the first contract scene*) Here's a pen. There's the door.

Wayland signs the contract. The boys are elated

Black-out

UNIT 24

Music

The applause and screams of an enormous Wembley crowd are heard

The Lights come up

The boys launch into an identical reprise of the song used at the very top of the show. The backing dancers are included in this number

Song No. 12 — Set Me Free

Curtain call

Following the curtain call, they present two reprise numbers. Band members may like to ad-lib a lead-in into the next number, such as asking the audience if they want more, etc.

Sean sings lead vocal in the following number. He sings directly to the audience. If possible, he goes into the auditorium and sings to individual women in the crowd. This is also filmed live by a camera operator so that the reactions of the females are relayed onto the video screen

Song No. 13 — Gotta Get You Home Tonight

The final number features the backing dancers. Towards the end of the number, the actors playing Robert, Mandy and Wayland join the dancing on stage which should build to a party atmosphere. The audience are encouraged on to their feet

Song No. 14 — Have Fun Go Mad

** Please note that an additional reprise can be added between songs 13 and 14. "**Driving Me Crazy**" can be performed again (if the song is being used) or any number from the show that is popular and upbeat.*

A second curtain call

THE END

FURNITURE AND PROPERTY LIST

Note: further dressing can be added at the director's discretion

ACT 1
UNIT 1

On stage: Setting of a concert arena
              Video wall
              Microphone stands

UNIT 2

Strike: Microphone stands

Off stage: Contract attached to clipboard (**Mandy**)

Personal: **Wayland**: pen

UNIT 3

Set: Cassette player

UNIT 4

Strike: Cassette player

Set: Three microphone stands

Off stage: Two microphone stands (**Laura and Debbie**)

UNIT 5

Strike: Five microphone stands

Set: Dressing for school toilets used as the band's changing-room

Personal: **Wayland**: van keys

UNIT 6

Strike: Dressing for school toilets

Set: Dressing for "The Rainbow Club" — London

UNIT 7

Strike: Dressing for "The Rainbow Club" — London

Set: Dressing for photographic studio
                   Cameras
                   Tripods
                   Flash umbrellas

Personal: **Wayland**: wallet packed with notes

UNIT 8

Strike: Dressing for photographic studio, cameras, tripods, flash umbrellas

Set: Dressing for television studio

Off stage: Radio (**Jay**)
                   Tour schedules (**Robert**)

UNIT 9

Strike: Dressing for television studio, radio

Set: Dressing for a hotel suite
                   TV set, with remote control
                   Video player
                   Video cassette
                   Radio
                   Telephone
                   Bottle of champagne and glasses
                   Plate of pathetic-looking sandwiches

Off stage: Huge bag of mail containing hundreds of letters — one containing a
                   pair of girl's frilly knickers; gifts including a West Ham scarf with
                   label and a diary; cards; cuddly toys including a Mickey Mouse and
                   a Teletubby with labels; photographs; an article from the *Daily Star*
                   newspaper. (**Robert**)

UNIT 10

Strike: Dressing for hotel suite, TV set with remote control, video player,
                   video cassette, telephone, bottle of champagne and glasses, plate of
                   pathetic-looking sandwiches, mail bag and all contents

Set: Dressing for TV programme
                   TV cameras (*etc.*)

Unit 11

Strike: Dressing for TV programme, TV cameras (*etc.*)

Set: Dressing for **Wayland**'s office
                   Desk and chairs
                   Telephone
                   Large rolled-up poster of an advertisement for milk. See description on
                       page 21

Personal: **Wayland:** watch

Unit 12

Strike: Dressing for **Wayland**'s office
                   Desk and chairs
                   Telephone
                   Large rolled-up poster of an advertisement for milk

Set: Dressing for recording studios
                   Earphones for all **the boys**
                   Three microphone stands
                   Sheet music for **Danny**

Off stage: Bottle of water (**Matt**)

Personal: **Jay:** twenty pound note

Unit 13

Strike: Dressing for recording studios, earphones, microphone stands

Set: Cassette radio player
                   Shopping bag containing hotel bed sheet

Unit 14

Strike: Cassette radio player, shopping bag, hotel bed sheet

Set: Dressing for hotel room
                   Bed for **Matt**

Off stage: A copy of the NME newspaper (**Danny**)

Unit 15

Strike: Dressing for hotel room, bed, NME newspaper

Set: Dressing for hotel lobby

Unit 16

Strike: Dressing for hotel lobby

Set: Camera

ACT II
Unit 17

On stage: Setting of a concert arena
                 Video wall
                 Microphones
                 Dressing for changing-rooms backstage

Off stage: Camera (**Photographer**)
                 Keyboard or piano

Unit 18

Strike: Dressing for changing-rooms backstage, keyboard or piano

Set: Desk and chair for **Wayland**'s office. *On desk*: piles of newspapers,
                 telephone

Unit 19

Strike: Desk and chair for **Wayland**'s office, newspapers, telephone

Set: Dressing for recording studio
                 Headphones for all **the boys**

Unit 20

Strike: Dressing for recording studio, headphones

Set: Dressing for canteen
                 Table and chair for **Matt.** *On table*: a drink

During lighting change page 41

Strike: Dressing for canteen , table and chair, a drink

Unit 21

Set: Dressing for a back stage area of Brit Awards venue
              Payphone

Off stage: Brit Awards trophy (**Danny**)

Unit 22

Strike: Dressing for a back stage area of Brit Awards venue, payphone

Set: Bits of rigging

Personal: **Adam**: pouch containing a small mirror and a tiny tin of cocaine

Unit 23

Strike: Bits of rigging

Set: Dressing for Wayland's office
              Desk and chair. *On desk*: The *Sun* newspaper with headline as
                  described on page 49
              Telephone

During the lighting change on page 50

Strike: Dressing for **Wayland**'s office, desk and chair, the *Sun* newspaper,
                  telephone

Set: Dressing for a meeting-room
              Five chairs

Off stage: Clipboard with contract attached (**Sean**)

Personal: **Danny**: pen

Unit 24

Strike: Dressing for a meeting room, five chairs, clipboard with contract
                  attached

Set: Camera

LIGHTING PLOT

Pratical fittings required concert lighting rig with moving lights; TV flicker effect

Act I, UNIT 1

To open: Darkness

Cue 1	Screams from Wembley crowd *Full concert lighting sequence — moving lights (etc.)*	(Page 1)
Cue 2	**Danny**: "... manager's eye ..." *Black-out*	(Page 2)

Act I, UNIT 2

To open: Black-out during video sequence

Cue 3	The screen fades out *As the screen fades, bring up general interior lights*	(Page 2)
Cue 4	**The boys** grab at the pen. **Wayland** smiles *Black-out*	(Page 3)

Act I, UNIT 3

To open: *Black-out during video sequnce*

Cue 5	At the end of video sequence *Bring lights up on rehearsal studio setting*	(Page 3)
Cue 6	**Wayland:** " ... at the bottom." *Black-out*	(Page 4)

Act I, UNIT 4

To open: *Dim lighting during school announcement*

Cue 7	**Announcer/Teacher:** "... premiére of — 'Freedom'." *Bring lights up to full*	(Page 5)

Cue 8   At the end of the song   (Page 5)
            Black-out

Act I, Unit 5

To open: General interior lighting

Cue 9   **Wayland**: " It's parked outside the school gates."   (Page 6)
            Cross-fade lights to focal spot on **Wayland** *and* **Mandy**

Cue 10   **Wayland** mimes ripping hair off his chest   (Page 8)
            Black-out

Act I, Unit 6

To open: Black-out during the video sequence

Cue 11   **Announcer**: "... give it up for — 'Freedom'."   (Page 8)
            Lights come up on the band

Cue 12   At the end of the song   (Page 9)
            Black-out

Act I, Unit 7

To open: General interior lighting

Cue 13   **Anna**: "Hold that ——"   (Page 11)
            The camera flashes several times in quick succession

Cue 14   The camera flashes several times, when ready   (Page 11)
            Black-out

Act I, Unit 8

To open: Black-out during video sequence

Cue 15   After the video sequence   (Page 11)
            Lights rise on the television studio setting

Cue 16   **Floor Manager**: (*voice only*) " ... ready, guys."   (Page 13)
            Lights focus on the boys

Cue 17   **Wayland** exits   (Page 15)
            Black-out

Act I, Unit 9

To open: Black-out during video sequence

Cue 18	**Matt**: "Yes I can." *Raise lights dimly on hotel setting*	(Page 15)
Cue 19	Video sequence fades to black-out *Lights raise fully on hotel setting*	(Page 16)
Cue 20	**Matt** hangs his head in embarrassment *Black-out*	(Page 19)

Act I, Unit 10

To open: Black-out during video sequence

Cue 21	Video sequence fades to black-out *Spotlight rises on* **TV presenter**	(Page 20)
Cue 22	**TOTP Presenter**: "... gorgeous — 'Freedom'!" *Full lights come up on the band*	(Page 20)
Cue 23	At the end of the song *Black-out*	(Page 20)

Act I, Unit 11

To open: General interior lighting

Cue 24	**Wayland**: "Good! Progress!" *Black-out during video sequence*	(Page 21)

Act I, Unit 12

To open: General interior lighting

Cue 25	**Matt** and **Robert** exit *Black-out*	(Page 25)

Act I, Unit 13

To open: General exterior lighting

Cue 26	**Wayland** walks away *Black-out*	(Page 26)

Act I, Unit 14

To open: General interior lighting

Cue 27   **Wayland**: "... thank me!"   (Page 29)
                 The lights cross-fade to a spot on **Wayland**

Act I, Unit 15

To open: Spotlight on **Wayland**

Cue 28   **Robert** and **Mandy** enter   (Page 29)
                 When ready, open spotlight to reveal **Robert** *and* **Mandy**

Cue 29   **Wayland**: " ... the world, haven't I?"   (Page 31)
                 Black-out

Act I, Unit 16

To open: Full concert lighting

No cues

Act II, Unit 17

To open: Full concert lighting

Cue 30   The band wave their way off-stage   (Page 32)
                 The lights cross-fade to changing-room setting

Cue 31   The photographer takes several pictures   (Page 34)
                 The camera flashes several times

Cue 32   **Jay** and the others exit   (Page 34)
                 Lower main lighting, bring up spotlight on **Sean**
                 When ready add further lights

Cue 33   At the end of song   (Page 34)
                 Black-out

Act II, Unit 18

To open: Black-out during video sequence

Cue 34   At the end of video sequence   (Page 35)
                 The Lights rise on **Wayland**'s *office*

Act II, Unit 19

To open: General interior lighting on recording studio setting

Cue 35	**Danny** walks off-stage	(Page 40)
	Black-out	

Act II, Unit 20

To open: General interior lighting on canteen setting

Cue 36	**Robert** exits, **Matt** is left standing for a moment	(Page 41)
	When ready fade lights slowly	
	Bring up dim spotlight on **Matt**	

Cue 37	As the video sequence ends	(Page 41)
	Open out spotlight on **Matt** *to reveal other band members*	

Cue 38	At the end of song	(Page 41)
	Black-out	

Act II, Unit 21

To open: General interior lighting on backstage setting   (Page 41)

Cue 39	**Danny**: "... Robert's number?"	(Page 45)
	Black-out	

Act II, Unit 22

To open: Black-out during video sequence

Cue 40	**MTV presenter**: "Watch this space."	(Page 45)
	General lighting comes up on the Wembley stage	

Cue 41	**Wayland**: "— get Danny back."	(Page 49)
	Black-out	

Act II, Unit 23

To open: Black-out during video sequence

Cue 42	At the end of the video sequence	(Page 49)
	Lights rise on **Wayland**'*s office*	

Cue 43	**Wayland** puts his jacket on	(Page 50)
	Black-out on **Wayland**'*s office. Follow spot on* **Wayland**	

Cue 44   **Danny**, **Jay**, **Adam** and **Matt** enter unseen   (Page 50)
            When ready, bring lights up on meeting room setting

Cue 45   **Wayland** signs the contract   (Page 53)
            Black-out

Act II, UNIT 24

To open: Black-out

Cue 46   Applause and screams from Wembley, when ready   (Page 54)
            Full concert lighting

EFFECTS PLOT

ACT I

Cue 1   To open, when ready   (Page 1)
Voice over dialogue as Page 1

Cue 2   **Voice over**: "— 'Freedom'!"   (Page 1)
Sound of screams and hysteria from Wembley crowd.
Special concert effects, pyros

Cue 3   To open ACT I, Unit 4   (Page 4)
Announcement delivered over school sound system.
Dialogue and description as Pages 4/5

Cue 4   At the end of the song. During Black-out   (Page 5)
Sound of hundreds of screaming girls

Cue 5   The video sequence ends   (Page 8)
Announcement for "The Rainbow Club".
Dialogue as Page 8

Cue 6   **The boys** sing the final lines of the song   (Page 22)
Studio intercom effect. Dialogue as Page 22

Cue 7   **Jay**: " ... what I just said?"   (Page 22)
Studio intercom effect. Dialogue as Page 23

Cue 8   To open ACT I, Unit 14   (Page 26)
The sound of female fans singing and screaming in street below

Cue 9   **Danny** goes over to the hotel window   (Page 28)
The crowd scream louder

Cue 10   **Danny** exposes his backside out of the window   (Page 28)
The crowd let out a great cheer and more screams

Cue 11   **Wayland** drags **Danny** away from the window   (Page 28)
Lots of booing from the crowd is heard

ACT II

VIDEO PLOT

ACT I

Cue 1   Band make their entrance   (Page 1)
Video screen reads "FREEDOM"

Cue 2   To open ACT I, UNIT 2   (Page 2)
Video screen shows advert in newspaper.
Description as page 2. Cut video screen at end of sequence

Cue 3   To open ACT I, UNIT 3   (Page 3)
Video screen shows a sequence of photographs and
video clips. Description as page 3. Cut video screen
when sequence ends

Cue 4   To open ACT I, UNIT 6   (Page 8)
Video screen shows **Sean**'*s practice test.*
Dialogue and description as page 8.
Cut video screen when sequence ends

Cue 5   During the black-out   (Page 11)
The video screen lights up.
When ready a video sequence shows a montage
of various studio shots. Description as page 11

Cue 6   To open ACT I, UNIT 9   (Page 15)
A video sequence shows a MTV or similar music show.
Dialogue as pages 15/16. When sequence ends cut screen

Cue 7   To open ACT I, UNIT 10   (Page 19)
A video sequence shows **Matt**'*s screen test.*
Dialogue as page 19/20. When sequence ends, fade screen

Cue 8   Spotlight rises on **TV Programme presenter**   (Page 19)
Footage of presenter transfers live on to screen.
Dialogue as page 20

Cue 9   Full lights come up on the band   (Page 20)
Camera turns to film performance live on to screen

Cue 10   At the end of song   (Page 20)
Cut screens

Cue 11   Black-out   (Page 21)
           A video sequence shows a series of milk poster adverts.
           Description as page 22

Cue 12   Black-out   (Page 26)
           A video sequence shows photos and video footage
           of the mass hysteria of the fans. Description as page 26.
           Cut screens at end of sequence

Cue 13   Second number of concert sequence   (Page 31)
           Camera operator films performance live so that
           it is relayed on to the screens

ACT II

Cue 14   To open ACT II, Unit 18   (Page 35)
           A video sequence shows a late night news programme.
           Dialogue and description as page 35.
           Cut screens at end of sequence

Cue 15   The lights slowly fade around **Matt**   (Page 41)
           A video sequence shows a presenter at the Brit Awards.
           Dialogue and description as page 41.
           Cut screens at end of sequence

Cue 16   To open ACT II, Unit 22   (Page 45)
           A video sequence shows MTV news.
           Dialogue as page 45.
           Cut screens at end of sequence

Cue 17   To open ACT II, Unit 23   (Page 49)
           A video sequence shows television breakfast news.
           Dialogue and description as page 49.
           Cut screens at end of sequence

Cue 18   **Sean** sings to individual members of the audience   (Page 54)
           The reactions of the females are relayed
           on to the video screen

ALTERNATIVES TO VIDEO PLOT

ACT I

Cue 1   Band make their entrance   (Page 1)
Projector slide reads "Freedom"

Cue 2   To open Act I, Unit 2   (Page 2)
Projector slide show advert in newspaper

Cue 3   To open Act I, Unit 3   (Page 3)
Projector slides show a sequence of photographs

The video sequence at the start of Unit 6 is cut from this alternative plot, and performances should start the unit from the **Announcer***'s dialogue page 8*

Cue 4   During the black-out   (Page 11)
Slide sequence of photographs

Cue 5   To open ACT I, Unit 9   (Page 15)
*Dialogue as pages 15/16 is presented as audio
only as though a radio programme. Exchange "MTV"
for the name of a popular radio station.*

Cue 6   To open ACT I, Unit 10   (Page 19)
Wayland *refers not to "Matt's screen test" but to
"Matt's audio test". It is on a sound cassette or
CD, rather than a video tape. Dialogue as pages 19/20.
Played in black-out*

The TV programme presenter speaks live in a spotlight on pages 19/20 ACT I, Unit 10 and footage no longer transfers onto video screens. There are extra lighting effects during **Song no 3 — Better Be Good***, page 20, to replace the filming of the band live onto the screens. After the song has ended there is a black-out*

The video sequence on page 22 showing a series of milk poster adverts is cut from this alternative plot and performances should proceed straight to ACT I, Unit 12 after the black-out

The video sequence on page 26 showing footage of mass hysteria from fans is cut from this alternative plot and performances should proceed straight to ACT I, Unit 14 after the black-out

There are extra lighting effects during the concert sequence, page 31 to replace the filming of the band live onto the screens

ACT II

Cue 7   To open ACT II, Unit 18   (Page 35)
              Dialogue page 35 is audio only and presented as
              though part of a radio show. Shown during a black-out
              or accompanied by mocked-up tabloid front pages on
              slide projector

Cue 8   The lights slowly fade around **Matt**   (Page 41)
              Dialogue as page 41 is audio only,
              played during a black-out

Cue 9   To open ACT II, Unit 22   (Page 45)
              Dialogue as page 45 is audio only and
              presented as though part of a radio show,
              during a black-out

Cue 10   To open ACT II, Unit 23   (Page 49)
               Dialogue as page 49 is audio only and presented as though
              part of a radio show; accompanied/followed by
              a sequence of photo, as described page 49

The filming of the concert sequence on page 54 is cut from this alternative plot.